Contents

* DECEASED

DANGERS
OF A PALESTINIAN STATE

EDITED BY

Raphael Israeli

gefen
publishing house גפן בית הוצאה לאור
JERUSALEM ◆ NEW YORK

Typesetting: Raphaël Freeman, Jerusalem Typesetting
Cover Design: Studio Paz, Jerusalem

3   5   7   9   8   6   4   2

Gefen Publishing House
POB 36004, Jerusalem 91360, Israel
972-2-538-0247 • orders@gefenpublishing.com

Gefen Books
12 New Street Hewlett, NY 11557, USA
516-295-2805 • gefenny@gefenpublishing.com

www.israelbooks.com

Printed in Israel

Send for our free catalogue

ISBN 965-229-303-2

Library of Congress Cataloging-in-Publication Data
Dangers of a Palestinian state / edited by Raphael Israeli
p. cm.
Includes index.
1. Arab-Israeli conflict – 1993– – Peace. 2. Nationalism – Palestine.
3. Palestinian Arabs – Israel. 4. Israel – Politics and government – 1993–.
5. Palestinian National Authority. I. Israeli, Raphael.

DS119.76.D367 2003 • 956.9405′4 – DC21 • CIP NO: 2002192865

Acknowledgements

THIS COLLECTION OF ARTICLES, authored either specifically for this publication or gleaned from previous writings of scholars or statements of politicians, is an attempt to take stock of the debacle of the Oslo process that began in late 1993 and finally fell flat on its face when the Palestinians undertook to achieve by violence what they could not attain through negotiations. Indeed, even when Prime Minister Barak of Israel stretched the Israeli readiness for concessions beyond the limits of what the Israeli public was willing to tolerate, notably at Camp David during the summer of 2000, and then at Taba after Palestinian violence had broken out, the Palestinian militants repeatedly vowed not to relinquish their age-old "armed struggle" with a view of squeezing Israel into submission.

The Israeli public, which for the most part had supported the peace process between Israel and the Palestinians at the height of the euphoria that followed the Oslo Accords, now felt disillusioned and abused, and began to put question marks on the advisability of adhering to those accords, which had come to signify that Israel must make continuous concessions while the Palestinians seemed committed to pursue violence. Therefore, while the Palestinians could get their state on a silver platter, as offered them by Barak in the summer of 2000, the Israeli public grew so disgusted by Palestinian conduct – which brought upon Israel as a result, death, misery and destruction – that it is less and less inclined to allow the rise of a rogue Palestinian state in its midst, that would turn the lives of Israeli into a continuous nightmare.

The contributors to this book – who understood this state of affairs before others, even before the Intifadah broke out, as they assessed the mood of the Palestinian people and its propensity for violence rather than reconciliation – have resolved to pool their knowledge and influence in order to apply brakes to the madness of Oslo, and to reflect on the consequences arising from a Palestinian rogue state. At the same time, being aware that the acute Palestinian problem required a solution, they produced a large gamut of ideas that could indicate alternative ways to address that issue, short of establishing a full-fledged Palestinian state in the West Bank and Gaza which, under the present circumstances, is more liable to cause friction than alleviate it.

The driving force behind the idea of putting together this book is the indefatigable Elie Yogev from Ramot Hashavim, who has single-handedly and with an admirable stamina and sense of purpose, elicited these contributions through endless nudging, and secured their publication in book form so as to alert Israelis in particular, and the world at large, about the inherent menace that a Palestinian state would pose to the entire Middle East.

Jerusalem, September 2002

Introduction

No one who participated in the Oslo process, or partook of its implementation, ever dreamt of its undoing in such a quick and dramatic way. The Oslo Accords had assumed that the PLO, being on the verge of extinction after the Lebanon debacle, the exile of the leadership, the dispersion of its armed force, and then its support for Saddam during the Gulf War (1990–1), would be grateful for the rescue buoy that Israel had launched, and embark on a new road that relinquished terror and embraced negotiations and peace. Therefore, it was believed by the Oslo negotiators that once the national rights of the Palestinians were recognized by Israel, and the PLO permitted to gradually gain control over the Palestinian territories that had been captured by Israel during the 1967 War, the Palestinians would behave like a responsible people, encourage dialogue and build the requisite trust with the Israelis that would encourage more concessions, in return for peace, tranquility and security.

However, no sooner was the Palestinian Authority installed in "Gaza and Jericho first" in 1994, and especially after the other principal cities of the West Bank were handed over to the Authority during 1995, that new terror operations against Israel were launched by Palestinians. Arafat at first denied the acts themselves, at times even accused the Israelis of mounting those acts themselves as "provocations". But then, in view of the escalation of the attacks and the rising number of Israeli casualties, the frequent exhortations of Arafat to his people to pursue the road of *Jihad*, and the shelter that the murderers found in the cities and towns under Palestinian jurisdiction, doubts began to mount in

Israel about Arafat's sincerity when he signed Oslo, and about whether he used those accords only to introduce a Palestinian Trojan horse into the Territories, as one of his "moderate" lieutenants, Faisal Husseini, was later to admit in a press interview.

Thus, under the cover of Oslo, which limited the Palestinian armed force in numbers and equipment, provided for the cessation of violence, for the arrest of terrorists, for the eradication of incitement and for the continuation of negotiations, in return for further gradual Israeli withdrawal from the West Bank and Gaza, the Palestinians created a new pattern of international behavior whereby they only clamored for the Israeli withdrawals to be pursued continuously and unconditionally, while their own obligations were disregarded and side-stepped. And when Israel demanded reciprocity, they insisted that they, being the weak and "occupied" party to the deal, deserved to be forgiven, pampered, helped and showered with money, while their stronger partner ought to evacuate the "occupied" territories without delay. So, instead of confidence-building, each step of implementation of Oslo created another obstacle, with Israel refusing to concede more assets as long as the Palestinians refused to implement their part. It also transpired that Arafat was unwilling or unable to move against the Islamic opposition to his rule – the Hamas and the Islamic *Jihad*, and found himself even incapable of abrogating the PLO Charter, or amending it, which would have signaled that the Palestinians had abandoned violence.

The Barak government, which was elected by Israelis in May 1999, on a platform of peace with the Palestinians, decided to move boldly in order both to test the limits of Arafat's sincerity and to put an end to the agonizing process of Israeli withdrawals that were not rewarded by Palestinian cessation of hostility, violence, incitement, harboring terror, smuggling weapons, corruption of the system and the like. With the help and backing of American President Bill Clinton, Barak and Arafat met at Camp David in July 2000, with the former offering on a silver platter an immediate Palestinian state in practically most of the West Bank and Gaza, in return for which the latter was to sign the end of the conflict between the parties. Arafat's agenda was different, which proved that his main concern was not to end "occupation", but to continue to undermine Israel proper, by demanding the "Right of Return" to the Palestinian refugees and their descendants, which would have meant the inundation of the country by Palestinians that would have drowned the majority Jewish population in a new Arab majority and turned Israel into Palestine. Arafat also demanded Muslim sovereignty over Temple Mount in Jerusalem, the holiest site of the Jews, thus depriving them of the focus of their identity and millennial longing.

When Israel did not bend, Arafat declared the armed Intifadah, where hundreds of Israelis were murdered, and double that number of Palestinians were killed or maimed in the retaliatory acts of self-defense launched by Israel. From the start, however, it was evident that while the Palestinians aspired to increase the numbers of Israeli civilian casualties, so as to cause Israel to break and relinquish its positions under fire, Israel sought to limit the numbers of Palestinian casualties by mounting surgical attacks and arrests among the Palestinian population of activists and terrorists. Arafat and his cronies responded by Islamikaze acts in which fanatic members of the Hamas and Islamic *Jihad* blew themselves up amidst crowds of Israeli civilians, causing massive death. In the months of March 2002 alone, some 130 Israeli civilians were killed and many more maimed. That is the reason that while Palestinian casualties are for the most part combatants or terrorists, Israeli casualties are mainly civilians and largely consist of women and children.

Arafat and his gang went one step further in their quest to drive Israel to despair and unilateral withdrawal. Islamikaze acts (that are popularly dubbed "suicide" bombings), which used to be the exclusive domain of the fanatic Muslims who were seeking their rewards in Paradise in endless sex orgies, now became the universally efficient mode of struggle, which was joined by the non-Islamists such as the Fatah's Tanzim and Aqsa Brigades, which are underlings of Arafat in person, in order to sow death and demoralization among the Israelis. A measure of the totality of the war that Arafat had in mind were the many cargoes of advanced and forbidden weaponry that were smuggled into the West Bank and Gaza, only two shipments of which were captured by the Israelis and made *cause celebre*. Tunneling under the Gaza-Egypt border, and manufacturing home-made missiles, rockets and light arms and ammunition, were other ways of ensuring a free flow of weapons into Palestinian hands and feeding the Intifadah. Arafat did not seem much preoccupied by the misery and suffering of his people as a result, as long as he and his cronies could continue to embezzle public monies, which were donated by Europe and the US for the functioning of the Authority.

It was these developments that disillusioned the Israelis, made many of them lose their trust in the "peace process" and choose the Sharon government, which had vowed to battle and eradicate terrorism and restore security to Israel. At the same time, however, realizing the casualties and damage caused to Israelis when the Palestinian Authority was allowed to turn its territories into bases of terror, most Israeli public opinion is now in favor of maintaining continued Israeli presence in the main cities of the West Bank, until security is restored to such a measure as to allow the final retreat of Israeli troops – once a responsible Palestinian government, national or local, takes over effectively. Until that happens, the international arena teems with ideas on how best to secure Israeli withdrawals from the West Bank and Gaza, how to restore peace and security, and how to establish some sort of Palestinian entity of evacuated land that would lead to a permanent settlement of the issue.

Differences of opinion abound in Israel with regard to the character of the entity to be set up in the final analysis. Some favor a full-fledged Palestinian state, like the envisioned one under Oslo, had those accords worked; others, who had believed in such a state, have had second thoughts since the outbreak of the Intifadah; still others, who had never believed in the positive metamorphosis of the PLO in the first place, now advance even more adamantly than before their arguments against a Palestinian state of any sort. Therefore, this book, which is the fruit of meetings, discussions, colloquia and personal and collective catharsis among the contributing writers of this collection, is an attempt to present to the public some facets of this new thinking, some of which derives from the lessons learned from the collapse of Oslo, with other aspects originating from traditional Zionist leaders who had concocted all sorts of plans and ideas that never came to fruition.

Yakov Hazan, one of the legendary leaders of the Mapam left-wing and pro-peace party, who had participated in a symposium in 1978 where he outlined his views about the clash of Zionism with Palestinian nationalism, opens this series with his memorable and prophetic remarks, which were made 15 years prior to Oslo. Abraham Diskin, a prominent political scientist from Hebrew University, who was shaken and awakened by the Intifadah and its ramifications, proposes a sobering analysis of the rapport of forces between Israel and the Arab world, as far as both demography and military power are concerned. When one realizes the findings of this analysis, one wonders whether Israel could, under the present circumstances of mistrust and enmity, relinquish the territorial assets that could mean its survival or perdition.

Mordechai Nisan, a foremost expert on minority affairs in the Arab world draws a very bold, but frightening, parallel with Lebanon, where social and political fragmentation brought about the disintegration of the Lebanese polity and its take-over by foreign powers. He envisages a situation of this sort to prevail if Israel were to ply to the demands to establish a Palestinian state west of the Jordan River, where the mixture of populations, ideologies, creeds, social customs and political convictions could wreak havoc on the very fiber of the country. Analyzing this prospect from a different angle, Arieh Stav, one of the foremost publicists in Israel, using a citation from the late Rabin during his time of sobriety and pragmatism, predicts the outright destruction of Israel should a Palestinian state come to pass.

Itamar Marcus, who has made a name for himself in his capacity as the founder and director of a Palestinian media monitoring set-up, presents the aspect of the role of ideological incitement in the make up of the minds of the Palestinian populace. It is agreed among researchers of political violence that rhetorical denigration of the rival/enemy usually precedes the battle against him, assuming, of course, that if the enemy is de-humanized, he becomes free prey for all. Under these circumstances of systematic cultivation of hatred by the Palestinian media against Jews, Zionists and Israel, no one can expect the Palestinian public in general, the growing generations of children in particular, to accept and respect their Israeli neighbors. A Palestinian state that lends legitimacy to this nurturing of hatred, can be no less dangerous to the Jewish state than a neighbor armed to its teeth.

David Bukay, a Political Scientist from Haifa University, and Michael Widlanski, a prominent journalist, analyst, commentator and columnist, both tackle the international aspects of the dangers that a Palestinian state would pose if it should come into existence. Both are scholars of Islam and the Arab world, but while Bukay deals with the key issue of the impact on such a state on inter-Arab relations, given the environment of support that Arafat expects there, and the internecine plots of which he is occasionally the victim, Widlanski addresses the vital issue of the impact on US interests, in view of the predominant role that the world's only superpower has had in the Middle East, as the patron of Israel and as an ally to various Arab countries in the region.

Having illustrated the multi-dimensional character of the dangers emanating from a Palestinian state, Part II of this book turns to possible remedies, which range from Palestinian entities at variance with the concept of a state, as currently demanded by the Palestinians and much of the world, in the West Bank and Gaza, to new concepts of self-determination where independence is not necessarily coterminous with statehood. Paul Riebenfeld of Columbia University lays the ground work of the *problematique* of statehood/s in Palestine, in view of the contradicting claims to it, followed by three alternative plans that were evoked by writers, regional planners and politicians over the past decades for the resolution of the Palestinian issue. The number of such plans amounts to dozens, but here only those three varieties will be presented, which the present post-Oslo turmoil makes the most likely to find followings and to gain constituencies in the West, if not in the Arab and Palestinian world, who would still opt for the elimination of Israel and the substitution of a Palestinian state for it.

The outline of Menachem Begin, the Prime Minister of Israel (1977–83) for an autonomy plan that would allow the Palestinians self-rule in their territories, while Israel retains the overall supervision of security, was on the negotiating table for several years, as Begin believed that in return for a peace with Egypt, for which he was prepared to concede the entire territory of Sinai, he could retain the West Bank.

But when the peace between Israel and Egypt was consummated, and even more so after Israel foolishly concluded a separate peace treaty with Jordan, which tossed the entire Palestinian issue into its lap, there was no escaping the reality that the problem demanded a national and territorial resolution, hence the irrelevance of Begin's scheme nowadays and the imperative to look elsewhere. Raphael Israeli of Hebrew University suggests two studies that might open new avenues. In the first, he examines ten options, ranging from autonomy and statehood to outright annexation of the territories by Israel, but concludes that only if the entire area of Palestine/the Land of Israel is taken as one unit, and its owners (Israel and the Palestinians) are led to negotiate its partition between themselves, will there be any hope of breaking the deadlock. Another alternative that he presents is based on Ra'anan Weitz's idea to divide the entire land west of the Jordan into cantons, which would be federated following the Swiss model, but would retain each its cultural, religious, ethnic and linguistic character.

Let us delve into the discussion.

Part I

THE NATURE OF THE DANGER

Zionism and Palestinian Nationalism

Yakov Hazan *was a leader of the socialist movement "HaShomer HaTza'ir" and also of the Mapam Party*

CERTAINLY, THERE ARE DIFFERENCES between the Arabs of the West Bank, the Arabs in the large cities of the East Bank, and the Bedouin on the other side of the Jordan. But in what nation are there not distinctions between urban and rural inhabitants, between farmers and nomads? And in what nation, particularly in more developed ones, are there not regional subcultures, areas that vary from one another in their local customs, areas in which there exist, beside the common national language, regional dialects – "sub-languages"?

The Arabs of Greater Israel find themselves in an accelerated process of national consolidation. The limits of this national-political consolidation have not yet been finally set. These limits will have a definitive influence on the nature of this national consolidation. The consolidation itself is a fact and requires no consent on our part. It is exclusively their prerogative. Here, our opposition would be of no avail, even if we decided, for whatever reason, to stand up against the process.

But the decisive question is: Do we have the right to exert influence on the establishment of the political framework for this national consolidation? In my view, it is a necessity of life. It is both a privilege and an obligation, both for our own sake and for the sake of the Arabs in the Land of Israel. And again: there is no symmetry here whatsoever. The national consolidation of the Arabs in the Land of Israel is assured, no matter what. The security of our national, politically independent existence obligates us to struggle against the establishment of an additional Arab state on the West Bank. The establishment of such a state will herald dangers and calamities both for us and for the Arabs.

The very existence of such a state would be directed against the existence of the State of Israel. Agreements and accords will not help, not even peace accords. Life here is more powerful than all of those. The spiritual father of such a state will be the PLO. Even if the majority will deceive itself, the Palestinian Covenant is not a political program that can be exchanged for another political program by a decision. It is a *Weltanschauung* and life belief. There will always be a segment [of the population] that will revolt against the majority and will carry on terrorist activities, both within and without, against us. Above this state will forever hover – no matter whether we are compliant or put up resistance – the shadow of the 1947 partition, and this will essentially delineate the political nature of its inhabitants. The establishment of such a state means the return to the original partition of the Land of Israel: Why only part of the [West] Bank – and even that only after border adjustments necessary for security – and not a return to those borders? Such a division into two states – Jordan on the east and Israel on the west – will result in a pressure cooker always liable to explosions, with such eruptions first of all directed westward, against us. It would not occur to any of us that it would be feasible to come to a peace arrangement without demilitarization of the [West] Bank. Is it possible to visualize a state that is completely demilitarized? Of course not. The [West] Bank, after border adjustments essential for security, will consitute only a part of a larger state. Is it possible to establish such a demilitarized state even against forces seeking to undermine its existence? Won't such a demilitarization serve as an incubator for terror organizations which, from time to time, will infiltrate the border – a border that is close to population centers in Israel?

As I was writing these lines, the "Voice of Israel" reported on Katyusha rocket explosions in a Jerusalem neighborhood. This was the third attempt to use lethal armament to disturb the peace of Jerusalem – and this at a time when the IDF still rules in Judea and Samaria. These aggressive weapons become ever smaller in size, even as their destructive power increases. It is easy to smuggle them in anywhere. A state that cannot, and essentially also does not want to, exercise control over "dissenters," with the excuse that it is not in its power to do so, will become a most dangerous springboard for the terror directed against us. The upshot will be that we will be forced to take matters into our own hands again, invasion will follow invasion, and so, in the eyes of the "enlightened" world, we shall become the aggressors, stifling an infant state in its cradle. Just what we need in our struggle against the isolation imposed on us from outside!

I do not contend that such a state should not be established because it will not be able to solve the refugee problem. Against this, it is possible to counter that industrialization will solve everything. True, industrialization of such a fledgling state, which, in addition to its other handicaps, lacks all natural resources, is not simple at all. And again they will retort: With money, everything is possible. But in my opinion developments will be completely different. And this possiblity makes me shudder. This state, completely permeated by the belief that it is only a transition stage on the way to the final political future – the establishment of a "secular-democratic" state – will gather within it all the refugees. It will keep them in camps set up close to the Israeli borders. And thus it will turn into a time-bomb, the inevitable end of which will be explosion. A third state in the region of the Greater Land of Israel will almost certainly lead to war in a very short time.

I am proud of the fact that there was a time when we espoused the establishment of a binational state in the entire Land of Israel. We did not want to resign ourselves to a division of the homeland, to which we have returned after a two-thousand-year exile. We believed in the possibility of a life of partnership and equality between the two peoples who live here: our people which returned to its homeland after long wanderings, and the Arab people who live here. These hopes were torn to shreds. Both inside and outside – around us – it was proven that this simply cannot happen. Reality has shown that the Jewish-Arab conflict can be solved only by the division of the homeland between its two peoples. This is painful to both nations, but for both there is no other way out, if we wish for peace. But this peace will be assured, if it is at all possible to achieve it in our generation, only if within the bounds of the Land of Israel on the two sides of the Jordan two states will be established, both independently viable, both able to deal with their internal problems – problems that can be solved within their respective areas – and both rejecting PLO terror which endangers or harms their existence.

Published in Hebrew in במה לבעיות חברה ותרבות בשער: *(At the Gate: Forum for Societal and Cultural Problems), Vol. 21, Sept–Oct. 1978, No. 5 (141), pp. 441–448.*

Waking Up from the Oslo Dream

Abraham Diskin, *Department of Political Science, The Hebrew University of Jerusalem*

EVER SINCE 1967 two propositions have dictated my view of the Arab-Israeli conflict in general and the Palestinian-Israeli conflict in particular:
(1) At the end of the road a Palestinian state will be established;
(2) There is no chance to achieve genuine peace between Israel and any of its Arab neighbors in the foreseeable future.

These two beliefs seem contradictory. Only a handful of extreme doves, who held that peace is around the corner, shared my faith in the first proposition, but rejected the second. Most hawks doubted the possibility to achieve an immediate peace and rejected the idea of major territorial concessions and especially the establishment of a Palestinian state. Today, even a number of very extreme hawks advocate the cause of peace and express the belief that peace can be reached 'under appropriate conditions' in the near future. At the same time, more and more Israelis – including hawks, who gave up the dream of greater Israel, and doves who realized the depth of the Arab hatred towards Israel – share my assessment that a Palestinian state is about to be established, while the achievement of real peace remains a dream. Nevertheless, given the lessons of Oslo and its aftermath, and especially given the vicious nature of the war that Israel is facing today, it seems that one should doubt any assessment and any proposed 'solution' of the conflict, including those mentioned above.

In the declaration of the establishment of the State of Israel, the Jewish leadership stated its hope of sharing the country with its Arab inhabitants, and for the development of peaceful relations with the Arabs. The declaration emphasized that "the State of Israel will be open for Jewish immigration and for the Ingathering of the Exiles; it will foster the development of the country for the benefit of all its inhabitants; it will be based on freedom, justice and peace as envisaged by the prophets of Israel; it will ensure complete equality of social and political rights to all its inhabitants irrespective of religion, race or sex; it will guarantee freedom of religion, conscience, language, education and culture; it will safeguard the Holy Places of all religions; and it will be faithful to the principles of the Charter of the United Nations." The first stage of the 1948 Independence War started long before the declaration was made. Nevertheless, the authors of the Declaration emphasized their desire for peace:

"We appeal – in the very midst of the onslaught launched against us now for months – to the Arab inhabitants of the State of Israel to preserve peace and participate in the upbuilding of the State on the basis of full and equal citizenship and due representation in all its provisional and permanent institutions.

"We extend our hand to all neighboring states and their peoples in an offer of peace and good neighborliness, and appeal to them to establish bonds of cooperation and mutual help with the sovereign Jewish people settled in its own land. The State of Israel is prepared to do its share in a common effort for the advancement of the entire Middle East."

As is well known, the Arab world never "missed an opportunity to miss an opportunity." It never accepted the very right of Israel to exist. The more moderate leaders in the Arab world were ready to accept reality and sometimes even to develop limited peaceful relations with the Zionist entity, but never justified the actual establishment of Israel. In 1964 – long before the Six Day War – the PLO was established, calling in its Charter for the total elimination of the State of Israel. The leading terrorist organization, Fatah, launched its first attack on January 1, 1965. The 1968 Charter of the PLO states that "Palestine, with the boundaries it had during the British Mandate, is an indivisible territorial unit" (Article 2). It declares that "Armed struggle is the only way to liberate Palestine. This is the overall strategy, not merely a tactical phase" (Article 9). The nature of this military struggle is explained in Article 10: "*Faday'ee* (i.e. terrorist) action constitutes the nucleus of the Palestinian popular liberation war. This requires its escalation, comprehensiveness, and the mobilization of all the Palestinian popular and educational efforts and their organization and involvement in the armed Palestinian revolution." The nature of Israel and Zionism, according to the authors of the Charter, is depicted several times. Article 15 states that "the liberation of Palestine, from an Arab viewpoint, is a national (*qawmi*) duty, and it attempts to repel the Zionist and imperialist aggression against the Arab homeland and aims at the elimination of Zionism in Palestine." Furthermore: "The partition of Palestine in 1947, and the establishment of the State of Israel are entirely illegal, regardless of the passage of time" (Article 19). Article 22 declares that "Zionism is a political movement organically associated with international imperialism and antagonistic to all action for liberation and to progressive movements in the world. It is racist and fanatic in its nature, aggressive, expansionist and colonial in its aims, and fascist in its methods. Israel is the instrument of the Zionist movement, and the geographical base for world imperialism placed strategically in the midst of the Arab homeland."

Arafat's many promises to change the Charter or to moderate it were never fulfilled, in spite of the theatrical act organized in Gaza for President Clinton, the establishment of ad-hoc 'constitutional committees,' etc.

The hostility of the Arab world towards Israel expresses itself everywhere. Israel was born in sin. On this point there is almost complete consensus in the Arab world, including Arab countries that have signed peace treaties with Israel and achieved friendly relations. The doves in the Arab world are prepared to tolerate Israel for lack of choice and, out of concern for the future, to renounce their previous aspiration to restore what was "stolen." But no one in the Arab world, including moderate leaders, is prepared to concede the justice of the creation of the Zionist entity.

Textbooks used in schools under the control of the Palestinian Authority routinely speak of the destruction of Israel as "the only alternative." In fact, the aim of destroying Israel is given prominence in kindergartens, grade schools, universities, mosques, the mass media, militant outbursts and official political statements. Ironically the word "peace" is interpreted by many Arab spokesmen as corresponding to "destruction of the Zionist entity."

Given the above, it seems that one should not wonder either about the nature of the present terrorist attack on Israel or about the reactions to the present military conflict throughout the Arab world.

While the discussion so far explains one's doubt concerning the possible development of 'real' peace, the question remains why under such conditions one may support the establishment of a Palestinian State. The main reason is that the essence of Zionism in our time is to ensure the continuing existence of a Jewish Democratic state. Already today, it is doubtful whether there is a clear Jewish majority in the land of Israel. To the 1.3 million Arabs who enjoy Israeli citizenship, one should add approximately 3.4 million Palestinians who live in the West Bank and the Gaza Strip. The following tables demonstrate that, on the one hand, Jewish majority "within the Green Line" was preserved thanks to massive immigration to Israel, and that, on the other hand, in spite of this immigration, the proportion of Jews in Israel is expected to go down in the future, due to the much higher natural growth among Arabs and to the fact that the massive immigration wave of Russian Jews is reaching its end.

POPULATION OF ISRAEL, 1948–1998

	Total	Jews		Non-Jews	
	Thousands	Thousands	%	Thousands	%
1948*	872.7	716.7	82.1	156.0	17.9
1958	2031.7	1810.2	89.1	221.5	10.9
1968	2841.1	2434.8	85.7	406.3	14.3
1978	3737.6	3141.2	84.0	596.4	16.0
1988	4476.8	3659.2	81.7	817.6	18.3
1998	6041.4	4785.1	79.2	1256.3	20.8

Source: Central Bureau of Statistics (1999), pp. 2–6
* End of the year data, with the exception of 1948 for which the date is 8.11.48.

SOURCES OF POPULATION GROWTH, 1948–1998

		Total Growth	Natural Increase	Migration Balance	Immigration	Emigration
Total Population	Thousands	5197.2	3018.4	2178.8	2737.8	559.0
	%	100.0	58.1	41.9	52.7	-10.8
Jews	Thousands	4192.5	2132.4	2060.1	2611.1	551.0
	%	100.0	50.9	49.1	62.3	-13.1
Non-Jews	Thousands	1004.7	886.0	118.6	126.6	8.0
	%	100.0	88.2	11.8	12.6	-0.8

Source: Central Bureau of Statistics (1999), pp. 2–8

Another demographic problem is associated with the questionable future of the Palestinian refugees. As is well known, not only the PLO but even the apparently 'moderate' Saudi 'peace plan' insists that Israel should accept the 'right of return' of Palestinian refugees. Implementation of such an idea will result in the appearance of not less than three states in the Middle East in which Palestinians constitute a majority: Jordan, the 'Gaza-West Bank Palestine' and the doomed-to-collapse Israel. The nature of this demand is quite clear from the following table that represents UNRWA figures.

1948 REFUGEES AND THEIR OFFSPRING
BY CURRENT PLACE OF RESIDENCE

Current Place of Residence	Absolute Numbers	In Refugee Camps (%)	In Other Locations (%)
Jordan	1,554,375	17.9	82.1
Lebanon	375,218	55.8	44.2
Syria	381,163	29.2	70.8
West Bank	579,987	27.0	73.0
Gaza Strip	818,771	54.7	45.3
Total	3,709,514	32.5 (1,203,828)	67.5 (2,505,686)

Source: *Ha-Aretz*, 23.7.2000, p. b3 (Based on UNRWA data for 31.3.2000. Excluding residents of other countries)

From all the above it is clear that, on the one hand, it is almost impossible to solve the "demographic problem" without the establishment of a Palestinian state. On the other hand, it is clear that the Arab consistent demand to fully implement the "right of return" is but another tool to materialize the intention to demolish the State of Israel.

One should bear in mind that a Palestinian state has never existed. In fact, most Arabs who lived in the country denied any 'Palestinian identity' until after the establishment of the State of Israel. Today, however, there is no question about such identification.

It should also be remembered that Israel is not threatened only by Palestinians, but also by the Arab world in general. How fragile the situation is, and how unjust the demands of the huge Arab world, one can learn from the following tables in which the size of the armies in the Middle East and basic features of different Arab parties are depicted.

SIZE OF ARMIES IN THE MIDDLE EAST IN 1983 AND 1994

Country	1983			1994		
	Soldiers (Thousands)	Total Number of Tanks	High Quality Tanks	Soldiers (Thousands)	Total Number of Tanks	High Quality Tanks
Israel	130	3650	600	136	3845	1930
Egypt	320	2400	1000	320	2800	1000
Iran	1000	1000	n.a.	340	1500	200
Iraq	875	3700	1700	350	2100	900
Jordan	70	917	230	85	1067	375
Libya	60	3000	1300	50	2710	360
Saudi Arabia	63	450	450	102	900	600
Syria	300	3700	2100	306	4800	1850

Source: Heller, 1984, pp. 260–261, Kam, 1996, p. 401. Similar tendencies, with different numbers, were published by other sources, such as *Janes* and the International Institute for Strategic Studies (London).

BASIC PROFILES OF ISRAEL, GAZA STRIP, WEST BANK AND SELECTED MIDDLE EASTERN COUNTRIES*

	Area (sq. km.)	Population (millions)	Density (population per sq. km.)	GDP (purchasing power parity – billion $)	GDP per capita (purchasing power parity – $)	Literacy (% of population over 15)	Life Expectancy (at birth – years)
Israel	20,770	5.9	286	110	18,900	95	79
West Bank	5,860	2.1	358	3	1,500	(90)	73
Gaza Strip	360	1.2	3,300	1	1,000	(90)	71
Egypt	1,001,450	69.5	69	247	3,600	51	64
Iran	1,648,000	66.1	40	413	6,300	72	70
Iraq	437,032	23.3	53	57	2,500	58	67
Jordan	92,300	5.1	56	17	3,500	87	78
Libya	1,759,540	5.2	3	45	8,900	76	76
Saudi Arabia	1,960,582	22.8	12	232	10,500	63	68
Syria	185,180	16.7	88	51	3,100	71	68

*2000 and 2001 estimates based on the CIA World Fact Book web site (January 2002)

The Arab-Israeli conflict in general and the Palestinian-Israeli conflict in particular remind me of a famous biblical story. Two prophets, Hannaniah, the son of Azur, and Jeremiah, the son of Hilkiah, held a public debate. Nebuchadnezzar, the king of Babylon, had just exiled the King of Judah. The question about which the prophets argue is when peace will return.

Hannaniah claims that peace will come within two years. "Amen, the Lord do so," responds Jeremiah. But he does not believe in an instant peace. "True prophets," says Jeremiah, "are those whose prophecies are about war, evil and pestilence." "Peace will come," he continues, "but it will take seventy years, not two."

The *Lebanonization* of Israel

Mordechai Nisan, *Middle East Studies,*
the Rothberg International School at the Hebrew University of Jerusalem.

T HE PALESTINIANS, as a particular regional community, constitute the sword of Islam and the dynamite of the Arab nation. More than struggling for national independence alone, the Palestinians have demonstrated their broader political goals. They fraternized with Third World liberation movements, embraced Afro-Asian peoples, collaborated with the Soviet empire, and hugged Islamic fanaticism. Yasser Arafat was the first international political figure to rush and bless the Islamic Revolution in Iran in 1979, hugging Ayatollah Khomeini in a brotherly embrace. In the Arab world, the Palestinians have served as the proxy of Egypt. As Arafat would claim, the Palestinian war represents "the revolutionary era" in the last fifty years of history. It is this motif, and Arafat's personal symbolism, which capture the essence of Palestinian politics, convoluted and esoteric though they be.

In 1980, at an Islamic Summit Conference in the Pakistani city of Lahore, a secret decision was taken that "by the year 2000 the Middle East will be [totally] Islamic and the Christians of the Orient and the Jews of Israel will be eliminated."* The one Great Islamic Republic covering the entire region has not, however, been established and there are Christians and Jews still living in the Middle East. But Christian

---

* Reports on the Lahore Conference appeared in *Mashrek International,* December 1984, p. 33; and *The Copts: Christians of Egypt,* vol. 17, nos. 1 & 2, January 1990, p. 3.

Lebanon is emasculated and under foreign occupation; and Jewish Israel is bleeding from Palestinian terrorism and targeted by neighboring Arab and Muslim states. The Muslim campaign to destroy Lebanon as a Christian homeland and Israel as a Jewish homeland reflects the intolerance of a world religion for other faiths, while demonstrating the determination and perseverance of militant Islam in carving out its glorious future.

But this Muslim campaign employs the Palestinian *avant-garde* of irrepressible struggle and unrestrained warfare to achieve the sweeping Arab goals of victory and conquest. Donning the mask of peace has never been an obstacle to single-minded Palestinian warfare.

The al-Aqsa intifada raging since late September 2000 is another chapter in the history of Palestinian strategy and struggle. Such a violent no-holds-barred terror campaign poised against Israel, its civilian society and military forces, has been pursued by the Palestinians virtually since the appearance of modern Zionism in Eretz-Israel. The explosive hate-filled conflict is more than one hundred years old. For the Palestinians, buoyed by a culture-mix of Bedouin plundering, Islamic *jihad*, and atavistic savagery, there is no inherent compelling reason to lay down their tools of violence. Death in sacrifice, with the dream of ultimate victory, is a higher reward than any conceivable alternative achievement or political scenario.

The history of the PLO in Lebanon provides a precedent for its present war against Israel. Indeed, the Lebanese case offers a model of struggle animating the PLO since 1993, when the Oslo peace accord would soon be transformed into the Oslo war. In Lebanon, from the late 1960s until Israel expelled 9,000 PLO fighters from Beirut in August 1982, the Palestinians employed a variety of means to overwhelm and conquer the native Lebanese society and state, to render them incapable of functioning effectively.

It is our intention here to summarize the past in order to gauge where Israel erred, and stress how she can recover, in confronting the contemporary case of Palestinian warfare within and against the Jewish State.

In 12 steps we shall succinctly demonstrate the unfolding *modus operandi* of the Palestinian struggle. If the existing intifada is *déja vu*, then learning from the past is central to the policy solution of the future.

1) By 1968, the PLO (as well as its various collateral organizations and movements) had established itself within Lebanon as an alien but autonomous Palestinian force. In the 1969 Cairo Accord, the Beirut government formally recognized the PLO as a contractual political entity. So too Israel officially recognized the PLO in 1993 with the signing of the Oslo Accord, and political symmetry defined this new bilateral agreement. The enemy was inside the gates with the foolish consent of the threatened state.

2) In Lebanon, the civilian Palestinian population of refugee origin, situated in and near the coastal cities, including Beirut, provided the armed PLO with a national and logistical base for its penetration of the country. This situation served as a legitimizing theme, suggesting that the civilian Palestinians required protection from the Lebanese authorities, now offered by their gun-slinging brothers. In Israel, the PLO entered Judea/Samaria and Gaza from Tunisia and elsewhere, ostensibly to provide security for the local Palestinian population against the allegedly predatory Israeli military forces. Thus, in both cases, a pseudo-democratic veneer of native Palestinian rule was presented as a just solution, when in fact what transpired was the denial of state sovereignty for Lebanon and Israel alike.

3) The PLO declared that, as ideologically twisted as it sounds, it wanted to establish a Palestinian state in Lebanon. This idea smacked of Arab revolutionary zeal combined with Palestinian national arrogance, with presumably a proviso that such a state would pursue the war against Israel in the heart of Palestine itself. For the PLO to call for a Palestinian state in the territories of the West Bank and the Gaza Strip, as a first step toward incorporating and thus demolishing all of Israel, is of course the essential political plan of the movement. In short, the PLO set out

to destroy two Middle East countries: Israel with its Jewish ethos and Lebanon with its Christian character. Sovereignty is to be reserved for Arab-Muslims alone.

4) In Lebanon, the Palestinians, numbering a few hundred thousand people, have established themselves as a major social presence in the country, especially in the southern coastal cities, including Beirut. This is a process of demographic conquest in urban neighborhoods that occurs despite their lack of Lebanese citizenship. Within Israel, Palestinians spread their presence throughout civilian society, in work places, on public transportation, and leisure park areas. In this way they occupy public space and intimidate the more sedate Jewish population.

5) The PLO became a political factor in Lebanese politics through the 1970s, especially after the outbreak of the Lebanese War in 1975. National politicians parleyed with Arafat in Beirut, and various Muslim, Druze, and Christian Lebanese figures collaborated with the terrorist thug as if he were a reputable statesman. As of the Oslo Accords of 1993, Arafat became a recognized partner in peace with Yitzhak Rabin and his prime ministerial successors. While courted by the sycophants from the Israeli left, the PLO leader acquired a stature within the Israeli public as someone who could either offer Israel security, peace and international legitimacy, or dismantle the Jewish state in stages, one step at a time. Israel became trapped in psychological servitude to the terrorists that it had armed with its own hands.

6) The PLO butchered, mutilated, and devastated its enemies, especially Christians in Lebanon, in a barbaric assault upon normal civilized life in the land of the cedars. Unbounded Palestinian violence struck at Beit Mallat, Chekka, Damur, and Ayshiyyah – and of course in Beirut the capital – across the length of the country in the 1970s. In Israel, from 1995 on, Palestinian terrorism ravaged downtown Jerusalem, Tel Aviv, and Haifa, Hadera, Afula and Kfar Saba, spreading from Nahariya in the north to Beersheva in the south, and a host of smaller villages and settlements in the territories. As much as the Palestinians were reli-

giously prepared to be martyrs in their holy war, they wanted above all else to hunt down and kill as many Jews (and Christians) as they could. The Muslim jungle had penetrated and wreaked havoc in the civilized zones of the Middle East.

7) The Palestinian campaign in Lebanon employed a variety of sub-groups and movements to carry out the multiple goals of the PLO struggle. Some factions, like that of Abu Musa, or *Sai'qa* under Syrian tutelage, did not automatically submit to Arafat's political authority. A tissue of confusion served to obfuscate the fundamental PLO responsi-bility for hacking away at Lebanon's social integrity and national sover-eignty. With the onset of the Palestinian intifada in 2000, the multiple terrorist movements that included an array of different Fatah-origin organizations, such as Tanzim and Force 17, and the Al-Aqsa Brigades complicated the political picture. Arafat claimed he did not exercise con-trol over all groups, and certainly not over the purely Islamic ones, like Hamas. This tactical maneuvering spread the guilt, diffused the process of identification, and deflected Arafat's responsibility onto lesser known persons. The arch-terrorist escaped trial, punishment, and death.

8) Despite embittered relations between Yasser Arafat and Hafez al-Assad, the PLO in Lebanon enjoyed Syrian support in the form of military and logistical assistance in fighting the Christians, and by Damascus providing a strategic shield from Israeli intervention during many years of fighting. Most specifically, the Syrian army stationed in Lebanon was during the 1970s a central geo-military pillar facilitat-ing Palestinian warfare across Israel's northern Galilee border. In the 1980s and 1990s, Damascus provided sanctuary for the Palestinian rejectionist and Islamic organizations in line with Syria's traditional ideological antagonism to Zionism. In concert with Syrian support for its Hizbullah Shiite proxy, the Palestinians also received assistance from this axis of power, which included Iran as well. Without the Syr-ian factor, Palestinian terrorism would have weakened considerably. Ten groups composing the Palestinian Rejectionist Front enjoy sanctuary in Damascus, which serves as their political headquarters.

9) The war of the PLO in Lebanon caused economic damage of unimaginable proportions. Bank deposits were transferred out of the country, commerce declined, industries were destroyed, professional manpower emigrated. Lebanon suffered a financial setback of two generations. In Israel, the Palestinian terrorist war brought the tourist industry to a standstill; commercial businesses, hotels, restaurants and auxiliary industries, suffered extraordinary losses. Rampant urban Palestinian terrorism, in Jerusalem, Tel Aviv, and elsewhere, created public panic that convinced Israelis to avoid night spots and entertainment sites. Before trying to eliminate Lebanon and Israel as political entities, the Palestinians first emasculated their societies and economies.

10) During the many years of fighting in Lebanon, the Palestinians never observed cease-fire agreements. Arafat signed hundreds of such accords, with no intention of keeping any of them. This political duplicity, rooted in a culture of cunning, ground down the tenacity of the adversary. Lebanese politicians became enfeebled from this barren exercise in conflict-resolution. In Israel, politicians incessantly called upon Arafat to observe the agreements he had signed, from Oslo in 1993 through the innumerable cease-fire understandings over the years. Arafat never fulfilled an agreement: he did not arrest terrorists (the foolish idea of "a terrorist arresting terrorists" lingered in limbo for years), extradite terrorists to Israel, or expunge hateful propaganda from the Palestinian media and educational curriculum. Israel became confounded with a political scoundrel whose pathological lying was normative in this trenchant "game of nations." Arafat promoted war, not peace.

11) The PLO artfully employed political doublespeak, in order to deflect guilt from its destructive actions in Lebanon and to blame the adversary, especially the Christian community. In the name of the "Palestinian Revolution" everything was sanctioned: fighting the Lebanese Army, attacking the Lebanese population, establishing a PLO headquarters in Beirut, utilizing Lebanese territory as a base from which to attack Israel. Regarding the al-Aqsa intifada, Israeli occupation of Palestinian lands

served as the legitimizing moral mantra for an all-out war ultimately designed not only to disrupt and cripple Israeli society, but to destroy the country as a whole, in stages, and with the active support of the international community along with Arab solidarity from within the region. Few were the states that objected or the instances of condemnation directed against the Palestinian war.

12) The PLO was successful in causing the mass flight of Lebanese civilians, overwhelmingly Christians, in the years of instability and breakdown throughout the country. Emptying Lebanon of its native Christian population was central to its Islamization and Arabization, which would bring to an end its historic legacy and national integrity on the Middle East map. The demographic and political transformation of Lebanon was part of Islam's war against Oriental Christianity, and the Palestinians were in the forefront of this historic campaign. So, too, is the PLO intent on driving the Jews from Israel by its war of attrition, against which Israel has responded with a lack of determination and clarity. For Palestine to be liberated from Zionist occupation, according to the sloganeering genocidal rhetoric, the Arabs have to overwhelm the Jews and compel them to flee abroad. As of this time, the PLO has not been successful in depopulating the country of its five million Jewish inhabitants. The Israeli Jews have shown resilience in remaining in their homeland, despite the Palestinian strategy to uproot them from their land.

While we cannot know what the immediate developments will be, the situation in the spring of 2002 is that the Lebanese model is playing itself out in Israel today. This demands of the government to destroy the Palestinian Authority and evict the PLO from the country. The Oslo Accords of 1993 introduced the Trojan Horse within the gates. Admitting this gross strategic error should lead to removing the existential domestic danger to Israel's survival.

Israel will not collapse as a functioning national entity. It is not, as PLO propaganda imagines, an imperialist outpost with no roots in the country. It is a solid national venture with a powerful state and military apparatus. The so-called Palestinian national struggle is, however, itself an appendage of Arab imperialism and Islamic *jihad*, without national coherence or historical legitimacy. It is destined to fail, collapse, and disappear. The Jews are not aliens in Eretz-Israel, while the Arabs are marauders and murderers who can cause suffering and damage, but cannot win the war.

The Palestinians in Israel hope to repeat Hizbullah's victory in southern Lebanon, which led to the shameful flight of the IDF in May 2000. At the same time, the Palestinians have adopted Lebanese-style terror tactics for their Gaza and West Bank campaign. The Lebanonization of the intifada uses religious symbolism and guerrilla methods reminiscent of Hizbullah warfare during the 1980s–1990s. Ambushes and car bombs are two typical Hizbullah methods that the Palestinians have employed throughout Israel, on both sides of the one-time Green Line. Encouraged by Hizbullah's victory, the Palestinians delude themselves into believing that they can also gain the upper hand over Israel. They can win battles, but not the war. The Lion of Judah may at times look like he is sleeping, but in an instant he can rise and roar and assert his rule over the kingdom.

Palestine on the Ruins of Israel*

Arieh Stav, *Director of the Ariel Center for Policy Research*

> *The principle of national self-determination,*
> *as proffered by the Israeli Arabs,*
> *is nothing other than an ideological cover*
> *for the constant, unchanging Arab demand*
> *to destroy the State of Israel*
> *and establish an Arab state in its place.*
>
> *Hans J. Morgenthau*

A. FOREWORD

The political process transpiring in the Middle East ever since the Madrid Conference (November 1991), and even more vigorously since the signing of the Oslo Accords (September 1993), is referred to by many as a "peace process" whose essence, as characterized by the US presidents George Bush and Bill Clinton, is the principle of "territories for peace." In other words, it is incumbent on Israel, the sole democracy in the Semitic domain, whose area totals 1/500 of that of the Arab countries, to divest itself of a commodity that it lacks, namely territory, while the Arab tyrannies must provide in return the sole commodity of which they have none – peace. From the standpoint of the State of Israel, peace for territory is a radical move that is liable to place the Jewish state on the verge of existential danger, since withdrawal to the

---

* A brief account, taken from: Policy Paper No. 73 (Ariel Center for Policy Research) from the book *Israel and A Palestinian State: Zero Sum Game?*, 2001 Ariel Center for Policy Research *(abstracted by Arieh Zaritsky)*

1967 borders, or to a line proximate to them, will return Israel to the
situation from which it was forced to stage a preemptive war so as to
liberate itself from the "Auschwitz borders," as Abba Eban characterized
them at the time. Today, however, the situation is far more grave than
on the eve of the Six Day War for at least four reasons:

a Israel is being pressured to embrace a time bomb – in the form of
   a Palestinian state on the outskirts of Greater Tel Aviv;

b The firepower in Arab hands and the range and accuracy of their
   weapons have grown immeasurably since 1967, especially in the
   realm of ballistic missiles;

c Since 1967 the ratio of the military balance between the IDF and the
   Arab armies has increased in Israel's disfavor from 1:3 to 1:5;

d The density of Israel's population has doubled, creating an unparalleled danger, in view of the escalation in the level of weaponry of
   mass destruction possessed by Israel's enemies.

For these reasons and many more, the Israel national consensus
totally negated the principle of "territories for peace" and withdrawal
from the Golan Heights, Judea, Samaria, and Gaza, until recently.

Meanwhile, however, some Israeli politicians have undergone a
180-degree about-face, and from a position of rejecting the return to the
1967 borders and a Palestinian state – along with what is referred to as
the "Israeli peace camp" – have transformed themselves into passionate
supporters of "territories for peace" and the establishment of such an
Arab Palestinian state.

Peres, for one frequently speaks of the "winds of conciliation and
peace that are blowing in the Middle East." In The New Middle East,
he foresees that "increase in the standard of living and the sweeping
economic changes will turn Gaza into the Hong Kong of the Middle
East." Peres' miracle will result from combining Saudi money and Israeli
technology. According to him, the "territories under Israel's control
serve as a stumbling block to peace by creating tension between the
Jewish state and its neighbors."

This paper analyzes the claims of the "peace process" supporters in
an unbiased manner, without self-deception that is so characteristic of
Jewish radicalism, which sees only what it chooses to see.

"CLASH OF CIVILIZATIONS": DOMINANT TRENDS IN THE MIDDLE EAST
Two central processes have characterized the Middle East over the past two decades and even more vigorously since the demise of the Soviet Union and the end of the Cold War, namely proliferation of the arms race and Islamic extremism.

PROLIFERATION OF WEAPONS AND STRUGGLE FOR HEGEMONY
Since the end of the Cold War and the dissolution of the Warsaw Pact, Moscow's former protectorates outside of the Communist bloc are mainly the Islamic countries: Iran, Iraq, Syria, Sudan, Libya, and Egypt. Excluding Sudan and Libya, these are key countries in the Muslim world that have declared aspirations for hegemony in the Semitic domain and are ready to achieve their goals by force.

The substantial reduction in NATO military expenditures threatened to bring about the collapse of the weapons industry. Subsequently, the Middle East was inundated with weapons from East and West, sometimes by pushing prices down below cost. The Middle East quickly became the focus of worldwide weapons sales. During the 1990s the region was purchasing 42% of world's weapons sales, twenty times the world average. Even if the Middle East does not go nuclear in the immediate future, the weapons in Arab hands are sufficient to neutralize Israel's nuclear deterrent and to create a locus of potential danger unparalleled since the end of the Cold War.

ISLAMIC EXTREMISM
Since the 1979 Khomeini revolution, Islamic extremism (often erroneously referred to as "Muslim fundamentalism") has spread from Iran into Sudan, Algeria, Egypt, Lebanon, and is thriving among the Arabs of Eretz Israel. Basically, this phenomenon is a spontaneous, authentic reaction of a unified, powerful civilization well aware of its massive scope of a billion adherents, that is anxious about the disintegration and loss of values in the face of globalization of Western values. Consequently, its two major enemies are America – "great Satan," and Israel, "the dagger in the heart of Islam."

Peres' assumption that "Islamic fundamentalism is supported by poverty, hence raising the standard of living will facilitate its demise" is unmitigated nonsense that lacks any basis in reality. This absurd assertion is an affront to any civilization about which people insinuate that it will sell out its values, moral ethos and cultural code for a "bowl of lentil soup" in the form of an increase in the standard of living in the Western sense of the term, namely "microwaves, Internet, porno, and soap operas," as the spiritual leader of the Hizbullah in southern Lebanon, Sheikh Nasrallah, described it. If there was any truth to this claim, Saudi Arabia, Kuwait, and the Gulf Emirates should be thriving democracies while Syria should be submerged in the darkest depths of fundamentalism, since their per capita GDP is 10-fold higher (and roughly equal to those of Western Europe). Needless to say, the diametrical opposite is true. Hafez al-Assad killed 20,000 members of the Muslim Brotherhood in Hama in 1982 out of concern about Islamic subversion, while violating the *Sha'ria* (Islamic law) in Saudi Arabia risks execution. Iran descended from a western-oriented country into the arms of Khomeinism precisely when its standard of living was among the highest in the region.

The trends described above seem to create a threat to world peace, more severe than that which prevailed during the Cold War era. Consequently, they arouse deep concern in the West. The "clash of civilizations" is not yet upon us due to the huge technological, military, and economical gap between the West and any potential Islamic coalition. For Israel, however, the situation is clearly different.

B. ISRAEL: "A PEOPLE THAT DWELLS APART"

The pinnacle of faith is the jihad.

The Arab world's long-standing effort to erase Israel from the map is anchored in a system of considerations intrinsic to the relations between the Jewish state and the Arab nation in general and Egypt in particular. As a result, *jihad* (holy war), as the overriding principle of Islam, and the long-term strategic interests of Egypt, form the dual basis for understanding the process of strategic abuse that is designed to force Israel's return to the 1967 borders, thereby facilitating its destruction.

THE ISRAELI ANOMALY

A practical ramification of the precept of *jihad* is the world's division between *Dar al-Islam* (House of Islam), the consecrated realm consisting of all the territories where Islam rules uncontested, and the rest of the world that has yet to be conquered and is therefore appropriately called *Dar al-Harb* (Land of Sword). *Dar al-Islam* ranges from the Atlantic Ocean to the Persian Gulf – an area twice that of Europe – in which every religious or national minority that has sought autonomy has been destroyed or oppressed.

Israel is the only non-Islamic sovereign entity in the spacious Semitic domain, and in all of their attempts to obliterate the Zionist entity the Arabs were routed on the battlefield – an unbearable, stinging affront to a culture that worships war as an ethos and violence as a principle. Consequently, Israel is an anomaly that refutes the *jihad* principle: despite its existence in *Dar al-Islam*, it is an extreme manifestation of *Dar al-Harb*. As a result, the standard sobriquets for the Jewish state, such as "a cancer in the body of the Arab nation" or "a dagger in the heart of the Arabs" might grate on the Israeli ear, but they are perfectly accurate from an Arab perspective. It is not Israel's borders that are the cause of the Arab hostility – a claim seemingly contradicted by the fact that Israel occupies only about 1/500 of the territory of *Dar al-Islam* – but rather its mere existence. The Palestinian Charter that represents the *jihad* principle in political guise, is also the canonized document through which the Arab nation comes to terms with the Israeli anomaly in the attempt to return Palestine to *Dar al-Islam*. Thus, the Charter proclaims the unity of nation and land, fundamentally rejects the legitimacy of the Jewish state, and calls for pan-Arab cooperation in the armed struggle to extirpate Israel. The Charter was never amended, not to mention abolished. The show staged in December 1998 for Clinton in Gaza was a cynical farce played for the media with his full consent and ridiculed by the Palestinians themselves.

EGYPT AND THE ISRAELI WEDGE

Egypt is the prime candidate to assume the mantle of hegemony in the Arab world, thanks to its population size (62 million), cultural primacy, and large army with state-of-the-art Western weaponry. Egypt's geo-graphic location, controlling the Suez Canal and the entrance to the Red Sea, grants it a clear strategic advantage, but the main obstacle to regional hegemony is its separation from Asia by the Jewish state, thrust as a wedge between it and the Arab nations to the east.

The Egyptian attempt to reach the Saudi oil wells through Yemen in 1963; the standing Egyptian claim on Eilat and the western Negev; its uncompromising position regarding Taba; the Egyptian media's persistent rendering of the map of Israel as "a dagger in the heart of the Arab nation" dividing the two parts of the Semitic domain, are testimony to this.

The Egyptian attempts to wipe the Jewish state off the map in 1948 and 1967 failed. Furthermore, as a result of the Six Day War, Egypt lost the Sinai Desert; in other words, its territorial geo-strategic asset and its launching point in its war with Israel. With the return of Sinai in the context of the Camp David agreements, Sadat – Hitler's diligent student and admirer, one of the most vitriolic anti-Semites in the Arab world and one who understood the inferiority complexes of Israel's leaders so well – conceived the long-range strategic plan to return Israel to what he characterized as "its natural size." Sadat internalized well the principle expressed by Shimon Peres when referring to the 1967 borders: "Without defensible borders, the country will be obliterated in war." This principle was reflected in the formula that Sadat repeated constantly: "It is incumbent upon us to return Israel to its 1967 borders; the remainder will be accomplished by the next generation" – leaving no doubt as to the nature of the objective resting on the shoulders of the "next generation."

Egypt's strategic goal is supported by a comprehensive, coordinated system of the following schematic tactical steps:

a Construction of a military force and preparations for war;
b Establishment of the "Palestine Liberation Organization";
c Political hostility designed to invalidate Israel's international legitimacy;
d Brainwashing and "anti-Semitic incitement of a scope unparalleled

since the late Middle Ages, the 'black centuries' of Czarist Russia and the Nazi era in Germany."

C. CONSTRUCTING A MILITARY FORCE IN PREPARING A WAR

With a per capita GDP of less than $1,000, Egypt is one of the poorest nations in the world. In 1990 it was on the brink of collapsing under a mountain of external debt that totalled close to $50 billion and equalled, at that point, its gross national product. Cairo was on the verge of declaring bankruptcy, when President Bush offered comprehensive relief of Cairo's external debt in exchange for joining the coalition against Iraq in Operation Desert Storm. The most comprehensive sweeping remittance enjoyed by any country since WWII totaled $29.5 billion, with a most convenient schedule for its debt payment. Egypt's cooperation with Iraq in developing weapons of mass destruction was "forgotten."

Egypt's economy remained totally ravaged as it was, and fertile ground for fundamentalism. All attempts at industrialization have totally collapsed, the government bureaucracy is the paradigm of ineffectiveness, sloth and massive hidden unemployment. Schools there furnish masses of ignoramuses for the non-existent labor market.

Egypt is the only country in the Middle East without any strategic threat to its territorial integrity. Libya and Sudan do not threaten Egypt and there is a peace treaty with Israel. Consequently, Egypt's situation since Camp David resembles NATO countries' subsequent to the dissolution of the Soviet Union. At the end of the Cold War, they cut their military expenditures significantly and set their defense budgets at 2% or 3% of the GDP. One would have expected Egypt to follow in their footsteps and direct its limited resources to enhance its citizens' prosperity. In practice, the opposite transpired.

The Camp David agreements deprived Israel of an important strategic/economic asset, the Sinai Desert. The Israeli loss was Egypt's gain as it received a most significant power multiplier. The prize for its willingness to receive Sinai was comprehensive American military aid totalling $1.3 billion dollars per annum, earmarked for the purchase of American weapons systems, and for upgrading its army based on

Western military doctrine – in other words, the elimination of Israel's "qualitative edge." Within a decade, Cairo's military expenditures skyrocketed and are now estimated at $14.7 billion dollars per annum – 28% of the Egyptian GDP (1997), characterising a country at war. There is no need to elaborate on what could be accomplished with an annual investment of more than $12 billion (the sum that Cairo would save if it appropriated its funds as the Western countries did after the end of the Cold War and according to its real strategic needs) as opposed to diverting such wealth to the black hole of the next war.

Syria's economic situation is even worse; its per capita GDP has dipped well below $1,000. Yet, like Egypt, Syria diverted all $5.5 billion that it received in the wake of its participation in the Gulf War to an intensive armament effort, especially in the realm of weapons of mass destruction and ballistic missiles.

A PALESTINIAN PROTECTORATE

The "PLO," "Palestinian rights," and the principle of the "Palestinian state," even if they are not Cairene creations from start to finish, are manipulated for its strategic needs in the struggle with Israel. The Palestinian state, when established, will be largely an Egyptian protectorate and a very significant catalyst in Cairo's aspiration for hegemony in the Middle East. Consequently, it is no wonder that the idea of a "Palestinian state" is greeted with blatant displeasure among the other Arab countries, which see through Egyptian intentions. Assad rejects this possibility since he considers "Palestine" as southern Syria.

The Jordanian opposition is obvious. The overwhelming majority (about 70%) of Jordanians are Palestinians. Establishing an independent state west of the Jordan will quickly lead, with Egyptian encouragement, to the delegitimization of the Hashemite dynasty. That is why the late King Hussein claimed that "Jordan is Palestine" and butchered Palestinians at every attempt at subversion. However, Israel's decision to recognize the PLO spoiled Hussein's plans, since Jordan could not allow itself to be perceived as less pro-Arafat than Israel. His monarchy had no choice but to join the bandwagon supporting the establishment of a Palestinian state with an Egyptian orientation.

The PLO, established in Cairo in 1964 before the Six Day War, was totally unrelated to the negation of the "rights of the Palestinian nation." Abd-el Nasser candidly depicted his establishment of the PLO as a tactical step, part of Cairo's long-range strategy for the destruction of Israel. Arafat is Egyptian-born, and the "Phased Plan", the political platform to destroy Israel, was adopted in June 1974 in Cairo under the direction of Sadat, who foisted it on the Arab League three months later. The "legitimate rights of the Palestinian people" is the phrase imposed by Sadat on Begin at Camp David. Arafat's decisions since Oslo have been taken in Cairo, under the close supervision of Mubarak.

The PLO has been assigned three functions:
a Terrorism, as murderous as possible, to bring about the decimation and demoralization of the Jewish public, in an attempt to transform terrorism from a tactical nuisance into a strategic threat;
b The establishment of an independent territorial entity in Eretz Israel to serve as a springboard for Arab countries in their future war, according to the Phased Plan;
c Negation of the legitimacy of the State of Israel by reducing it to the partition borders on the basis of UN Resolution 181.
Arafat has completely achieved his first objective, most of the second, and is energetically striving to implement the third objective.
a *Terrorism: From Tactical Nuisance to Strategic Threat*
Israel is the first country in the modern era to capitulate to terrorism and act according to its dictates. During two years, from September 13, 1993, when Oslo I was signed, to the signing of the interim agreement (Oslo II) on September 28, 1995, Arab terror claimed more than 38% of all the victims of Arab terror in the history of Israel. The 21st century's terror is even more dramatic.
b *The Phased Plan*
The Phased Plan was adopted by the Palestinian National Council (PNC) in Cairo in June 1974. The crucial section, as defined by paragraph 8 of the plan, stipulates that: "Once it is established, the Palestinian National Authority (PA) will strive to achieve a union of the confrontation countries, with the aim of completing

the liberation of all Palestinian territory, and as a step along the road to comprehensive Arab unity."

As a constitutional decision obligating the PNC, the Phased Plan is unceasingly mentioned in speeches delivered by Arafat and other leaders of the PA. Arafat's demands have already greatly exceeded the territories of Judea, Samaria, and Gaza as they were pledged in the Oslo agreements, and they now call for forcing Israel to the partition borders. The Wye agreement transferred all of Judea, Samaria, and Gaza to Arafat. Hence the Arabs have achieved the basic objective of the Phased Plan, and the formal confirmation will follow soon.

c *Political Delegitimization*

The negation of Israel's legitimacy in its present borders is not a product of Israel's "conquest" during the Six Day War, but rather of its "conquests" in 1948. The only borders recognized by the international community are the partition borders of November 1947 (UN Resolution 181).

On March 21, 1999, Arafat met UN Secretary-General Kofi Annan demanding to convene the General Assembly to discuss Israel's violations of Resolution 181. On April 28, 1999, the PNC demanded to establish a Palestinian state within the partition borders and to comply with UN Resolution 194 of December 1948 concerning the right of Palestinian refugees to return to their homes.

The European Union soon afterwards declared its support for the Arab demand. As a preliminary gesture of goodwill to Arafat, the German ambassador in Israel publicized a demand to internationalize Jerusalem by transforming it into a *corpus separatum*, based on the partition borders. The UN Human Rights Commission passed a resolution in its annual session in Geneva (April 27, 1999), calling for self-determination for the Palestinian nation on the basis of UN Resolution 181, and demanded that Israel comply with Resolution 194.

On July 2, President Clinton announced that "the refugees should be able to settle wherever they want to live," i.e., flooding the Jewish state with millions of Arabs. On July 15, the UN General Assembly adopted a sweeping resolution accusing Israel of violating the 4th Geneva Convention forbidding the transfer of population to occupied territories. The reference was to all occupied territories, that is including those "occupied" in 1948. Resolution 181 is repeatedly mentioned in UN documents. Based on this exact principle, the Arab League, led by Egypt, raised the issue of 181 in its session in early September and demanded that the UN implement it forthwith.

Thus, the political process called in Orwellian fashion the "peace process," constitutes the diametric opposite in terms of its consequences for Israel's circumstances and interests, which, as always, relate to the very roots of the Jewish state's existence.

STRATEGIC ABUSE

The grave process described above has its origins in a series of circumstances. Some are objective, e.g. the loss of Israel's status as a strategic asset of the United States in the Middle East with the collapse of the Soviet Union. Some are intrinsic to the national ethos of the Jewish people, such as their exceptional talent for self-deception. Both of these manifest themselves in the process of strategic abuse that Israel has been undergoing over the past decade.

Strategic abuse transpires when a nation collapses under the critical mass of an external threat with which it is unable to cope. In this situation, the spiritual and physical purpose of national existence, disintegrates. From a certain point, a process of self-destruction begins that manifests itself in gradually worsening stages of demoralization, eventually leading to collaboration with the enemy.

The enemy, if he is sophisticated enough, will not take any radical action, i.e., war, but instead completely utilizes the strategic abuse in order to minimize the danger posed by the designated victim, until all that is left of the threatened country is an empty shell. At that point, there is usually no need to use force. The exhausted entity, which has lost its existential purpose and survival instinct, falls into the enemy's hands like ripened fruit. This schematic description, which is designed to evoke memories of the elimination of Czechoslovakia from the map on March 15, 1939, is transpiring before our very eyes, albeit more slowly, in today's Jewish state, under the semantic euphemism "land for peace," a phrase that never left Hitler's lips so long as he had yet to acquire all of the territories that he demanded.

In this situation, the principle of "mental block" emerges, which means selective vision regarding the enemy's intentions, misinterpretation of reality, and a compulsive addiction to the mantra of "peace" in the hope that the mere mention of it will transform it from ideal to reality. The following is but one of many examples:

Addressing an assembly of the Jerusalem branch of the Fatah Youth (on November 15, 1998), Arafat spoke of the impending establishment of the Palestinian state, emphasizing that he meant the entire "Palestine," whose capital is Jerusalem and which he "will defend with rifles." Arafat quoted a verse from the Qur'an in which Allah decreed "destruction upon the Children of Israel", and repeatedly mentioned the "Hudaibiya peace," which symbolizes the deception of the enemy through signing of a false peace treaty. The Fatah constitution was distributed to the participants in the assembly, noting that it is the constitution of the Palestinian state to be established. It explicitly declares that the supreme objective is "destruction of the Zionist presence in Palestine." All of the PA newspapers published Arafat's speech in great detail, and excerpts were published in the Hebrew press.

The Ariel Center sent a copy of Arafat's speech, a blatant declaration of war and a grotesque violation of the agreements signed by the PA, together with the Fatah constitution, to the Prime Minister's Office and to the central committees of all of the political parties. No reaction came from PM Netanyahu. The Labor Party declared that Arafat's remarks were intended for internal consumption, and Meretz asserted that Arafat's remarks were not different from statements made by the Israeli right demanding all of Jerusalem (*sic*) and all of Eretz Israel. The other parties (Likud, National Religious Party, Yisrael Ba'aliya, Third Way, Gesher), Moledet excluded, were clueless concerning the topic in question. A typical response came from the Foreign Ministry:

"What's the big deal? We've heard much worse things from Arafat in the past."

As mentioned above, the objective of the strategic abuse, referred to as the "peace process," is to bring about Israeli withdrawal to the 1949 cease-fire lines as a first step toward its physical liquidation. If this next step is consummated, what will be the results?

D. THE PRICE OF WITHDRAWAL

Without defensible borders the state will be obliterated in war.

Shimon Peres

Until recently, this emphatic pronouncement by Shimon Peres was a fundamental tenet of Israel's strategic thinking, and its ramifications go far beyond the military. It is a tapestry interwoven from numerous components that together constitute the price Israel will be forced to pay for allowing the establishment of a Palestinian state. Loss or concession of any of these components separately would result in a grave but manageable threat. Their combination into one aggregate will place Israel on the verge of existential danger. The Palestinian state is intended to serve as a launching point for a comprehensive war. Israel's ceding of the so-called "West Bank" will encourage the Moslem world to initiate a war that will be regarded by them as "the final blow to the Jewish entity" in the Middle East.

Liberating portions of the homeland in the Six Day War provided Israel with a power multiplier of decisive significance in the form of territorial strategic assets without which it will not be able to exist. Immediately after the war, President Johnson received from the head of the Joint Chiefs of Staff, Gen. Wheeler, a map of the minimal borders required for Israel's survival, that served as the basis for the definition of "secure and recognized boundaries" in UN Resolution 242 of November 1967. It includes most of Judea and Samaria, all of the Golan Heights (before the evacuation of Kuneitra in 1974), in addition to 5,000 square kilometers in Sinai that would enable the defense of Eilat and give Israel control of the entrance to the Red Sea in Sharm e-Sheikh. Thus, Israel possesses already less than the minimal territory required for its defense, as determined 35 years ago. Withdrawal from the remaining territorial assets to the 1967 borders, especially considering the present levels of armaments in the Arab world, will rob Israel of the ability to defend itself. The details of the strategic and logistic challenges confronting the IDF, if it is required to withdraw from Judea, Samaria, Gaza, and the Golan Heights, and of the dangers facing Israel are enough to fill a thick volume. Withdrawal to the 1967 borders will collapse Israel's military doctrine concerning the future battlefield, according to which western Israel and the Golan are one organic unit.

From a purely logistical perspective, with the population density in Israel, there is insufficient space for the deployment of the army at its present size, not to mention firing ranges and training areas. The ground-based early warning capability, a decisive component of the army's readiness in case of a surprise attack, will be critically diminished due to the topography of the area. The airborne alternatives (AWACS or J-STAR platforms) can offer only a partial early warning capability alongside ground facilities, and these are so expensive and vulnerable that, in terms of cost effectiveness and in light of the topography and the surface of Eretz Israel, it is doubtful they could prove effective. Withdrawal to the 1967 borders and the establishment of a Palestinian state will undermine the balance of power between Israel and its immediate neighbors. This situation will "arouse an uncontrollable desire within the Arabs to destroy Israel," according to Shimon Peres as quoted above.

In addition to losing strategic military assets, withdrawing from the so-called "West Bank" will cause Israel heavy losses in its moral status, nuclear deterrence and water supply, as well as American support (reduced to a strategic burden rather than an asset).

E. THE PALESTINIAN STATE

In Oslo, the Israeli government signed an agreement with an organization that remains committed to the destruction of the State of Israel. This goal is overt in all of the PLO's public expressions and pronouncements: 1. in the very character of *jihad*; 2. by dint of its name: the "Palestine Liberation Organization"; 3. in its constitution, the "Palestinian Charter"; 4. in its political platform, the Phased Plan, which depicts the state as a first step on the road to destroy Israel; 5. in the Fatah Constitution which is the dominant body of the embryonic Palestinian state and its anticipated ruling party; and 6. in its emblem, which is the map of the entire Eretz Israel with no vestige of the Jewish state. Immediately upon its establishment, the Palestinian state will act according to its constitutional, political, and ethical obligations, taking the following steps:

a *Geography:* A declaration will be issued that announces the inclusion of all of Judea, Samaria and Gaza in the Arab Palestinian nation with Jerusalem as its capital. These are indeed the geographic dimensions of the Palestinian state as depicted in the Oslo Accords, and the entire world, led by the United States, will salute the declaration, hence Israel will have no choice but to accept the decision.

b *Military Cooperation:* To neutralize Israel's decisive superiority, agreements will be signed with Arab countries, resulting in a comprehensive armament program. Israel will be powerless to do anything about it because international law allows a sovereign country to sign strategic cooperation agreements and military treaties with whomever it pleases.

c *Building an Army:* Arafat will announce mandatory conscription. The present core of the PLO army, estimated at 50,000 soldiers, has an additional 20,000 terrorists among the "Rejectionist Front" organizations in Syria, Lebanon and Iraq who will arrive in Judea, Samaria and Gaza immediately upon establishing the state. The PA can draft at least 100,000 more men through mandatory conscription. This significant force of over 160,000 men in uniform (roughly equaling Israel's regular army), built up within a few years and deployed on the outskirts of Greater Tel Aviv, will not require tanks nor fighter planes in order to constitute a grave threat to Israel's soft underbelly. Without even firing one shot, they will force the IDF to deploy massive forces so as to neutralize the Palestinian threat.

At this point, Egypt will once again raise its demand to evacuate all foreign forces from Sinai, as mandated by international law and in the same way as on the eve of the Six Day War. The evacuation of the international force will compel the IDF to mobilize and deploy substantial forces on Israel's southern border.

The withdrawal from the Golan will lead to the encirclement of Israel's north from Rosh Hanikra to the Kinneret by the Syrian army. Israel will be unable to deploy its small regular army along all the borders, the length of which will double from its present dimension, as will be required according to the above scenario.

The military balance of regular forces from the "inner circle" threat, including Syria, Egypt, and the Palestinian state, will be 5:1. When Jordan will sense Israeli vulnerability, it will join the threatening forces, as will Saudi Arabia, Iraq, Libya and Iran. In this situation, without the need to fire even one shot, the strategic abuse of Israel will reach a new level, which will manifest itself in a new series of ultimatums such as dismantling its nuclear potential and autonomy for the Israeli Arabs. The alternative to Israeli acquiescence to these demands will be all-out war under conditions of an unfavorable balance of military forces.

F. AFTERWORD

HISTORIC WINDOW OF OPPORTUNITY AND HOW TO MISS OUT ON IT

The megatrends in the Middle East described above provide Israel with a rare historic window of opportunity. The most dangerous process from a global perspective is the intensification of Islamic hegemony – a nationalist civilization motivated by imperialist, religious aspirations and armed with weapons of mass destruction and means to deliver them. Israel is in the eye of the storm, but not alone. Turkey is concerned about Arab-Iranian subversiveness and its influence on the country's Muslim majority, which is liable to bring the Ataturk revolution and the secular government to an end. Syria is a common enemy, and Turkish-Israeli strategic cooperation clearly would neutralize the Syrian threat (as well as the long-term Iraqi threat). The common interest has created an intricate network of ties between the two countries on the basis of military cooperation, especially in the area of upgrading weapons systems, missiles, and military technology.

India is an additional, extremely important objective for military/ economic cooperation with Israel. The large Muslim minority in India and Islamic subversiveness stand at the top of the priorities list on the Indian subcontinent. Like Turkey, India is a potential market for Israeli military technology. Cooperation between India and Israel in the field of computers, in which area both are among the world centers, could aid the Indian economy and rescue it from the Third World status in which it is mired.

A strategic triangle of India, Israel, and Turkey could create a very powerful center in the Middle East that could contribute much to undermine Islamic hegemony. Strategic power centers naturally attract other interested parties. Ethiopia, Nigeria, and Kenya are natural candidates. Halting Islam would have a salubrious effect on democratic tendencies, weak and modest as they may be, in the Arab countries themselves. So, for example, the possibility that Iran, in which the processes of recovery from Khomeinism are beginning, might join the coalition in the future cannot be ruled out. The process of liquidating minorities in the region, especially Christians, would cease or at least be mitigated.

The effect such a turn of events would have on the Jewish state's standing in the international arena is easy to imagine. As part of a powerful strategic treaty, Israel would cease to be the trampled doormat of the European community, that is located within ballistic-missile range of Arab countries. Likewise, they are threatened by Muslim irredentism in their own lands: the Muslim minority in France now constitutes 10% of the population and continues to grow rapidly. Europe is aware of the Islamic threat. The Europeans, who have a well-developed historical memory, do not forget that the defeat of Richard the Lionheart by Saladin at the end of the 12th century brought Islam to the gates of Vienna by the 17th century. Consequently, Europe is a natural ally for Israel. In order to achieve this, however, Israel must project power, resolve, and strategic backing of other regional powers such as India and Turkey.

With the dissolution of the Soviet Union, the US Congress became the most significant power center in the world. In contrast to the president who represents short-term American interests, if for no other reason than the time limitations of his term in which he must produce immediate results, the strategic thinking of Congress is long-term, which accounts for the basic difference in their respective attitudes toward Israel. US Presidents Bush and Clinton pursued a policy of dismemberment of Israel and its relegation to the 1967 borders. By contrast, a sweeping majority in the Congress – the authentic representative of the American public – adamantly opposes this policy, because a strong Israel with safe borders is a clear American interest. There is no more blatant manifestation of the polarization between the White House and Congress than the issue of Jerusalem. Whereas both houses of Congress decided by an overwhelming majority to transfer the American embassy from Tel Aviv to "Jerusalem – united forever under Israeli sovereignty" (in the bill's language!), President Clinton, with the cooperation of Rabin, Netanyahu, and Barak, vetoed the bill. The issue of Jerusalem, of course, with its symbolic and historical significance, involves far more than the geographic location of the embassy. Without a doubt, American recognition of a united Jerusalem as Israel's capital would halt, and possibly even terminate, the "peace process," and that was precisely the Washington lawmakers' intent. On the other hand, the White House's obvious goal of dividing Jerusalem is what will return Israel to the 1967 borders.

Thus, with the collapse of the Soviet Union and the end of the Cold War, a historic window of opportunity opened for Israel. Actual implementation of the present disastrous political process – designed to emasculate the Jewish state and transform it from a regional power to a divided entity on the threshold of existential demise – would seal the window of opportunity forever. What possible interest could Turkey or India have in a shriveled Israeli entity with suicidal tendencies that cooperates with its most heinous enemies? Historical precedent teaches that the political anti-Semitic tendencies of the European Union will continue to develop. The US Congress, the last stronghold supporting Israel, will abandon it as well. And the abandonment will be justifiable, since one cannot expect the average congressman or senator to be more Zionist than the Israelis themselves.

The patient reader who has reached this point, especially the reader upset by the air of pessimism permeating this article, will certainly ask: What can Israel do to escape the murderous trap into which it has fallen? The answer was provided in a 1997 document (the Declaration of Intent of the Ariel Center for Policy Research). The following are the main points:

"Defining of an alternative political-diplomatic strategy is conditioned first and foremost on acceptance of the basic assumption that the goal of the Arab world is to reduce Israel to the 1949 lines in order to make it easier to destroy the Jewish state. Therefore, consummation of the "peace process" means certain war, and this would take place under conditions, topographical and strategic, of decisive Israeli inferiority.

On the other hand, if the process is stopped now, the probability of war, though still very high, is not absolutely certain. And if war does break out, Israel's chances of winning will be immeasurably higher in the present borders.

Hence, stopping the process is an existential necessity for Israel.

It is true that withdrawing from the "peace process" would mean paying an international political price. However, this price, high as it might be, would be immeasurably preferable to the existential danger entailed in retreat to the 1949 lines.

Israel will have to struggle in four arenas at one and the same time. This is to be done while conducting an aggressive, unceasing information campaign that corresponds to a variety of relevant target audiences. The purpose would be to achieve world understanding of Israel's history, rights, and needs, in order to combat effectively the multiform and multitudinous Arab fabrications and inventions. To accomplish this, a government information agency needs to be established.

The four arenas of struggle that policy makers will have to deal with are as follows:

1 *The Possibility of War*

One must assume that the Arab world will not come to terms with an Israeli decision to freeze the present situation and to stop "the momentum meant to restore Israel to its natural size," as Anwar Sadat put it. Therefore, a high probability of war exists, and Israel must be ready to face it. For that purpose, the IDF must recover its deterrent image, which has been severely damaged, and a military doctrine must be clearly defined to deal with the anticipated conflict, which will consist mainly of the enemy's launching of surface-to-surface missiles at Israel's home front.

Tough deterrence: a. Israel possesses strategic assets in Judea-Samaria and the Golan; b. the techno-scientific gap between Israel and its enemies is considerable; c. the level of armament in weapons of mass destruction in the Arab states has not yet reached the stage of critical mass. In combination, these factors might deter the Arabs from an adventure that they could perceive to be very dangerous.

However, if deterrence does not work, Israel must deploy for the possibility of a preventive war and, in contrast to the past, clearly define the strategic/diplomatic/political goals of the war.

2 *The European Union*

The political-diplomatic cost to Israel's relations with the member-states of the European Union might be heavy and even involve economic sanctions. However, a combination of determination on the one hand, and a comprehensive information campaign on the other, might soften European hostility. This will work chiefly if the European Union internalizes the fact that Israel has enduring principles of national defense that it will not violate even at the cost of a general war.

In the information campaign Israel must make it very clear that we have learned our lessons well from the example of Czechoslovakia and the Munich Agreement, and that there is no chance that

Israel will commit suicide on the altar of European appeasement. On the contrary, just as Czechoslovakia's power vis-à-vis the Nazi threat was the keystone of peace in Europe in the late 1930s, so now Israel's power facing the Islamic threat is in the paramount interest of the Western world.

3 *Relations with the United States*

The diplomatic-political cost to relations with the US might be lower than we customarily think. Israel has many allies in both houses of Congress, in the military establishment, among Christian fundamentalists, and the broad public. The fact is that whenever Israel made clear that there was a clash of interests between it and Washington and stood resolutely for its position, it was able to hold its ground. Three examples: application of Israeli law and administration to the Golan; Jerusalem Law; destruction of the Iraqi nuclear reactor.

4 *The Internal Israeli Arena*

The public in Israel is obliged to pay the price of both peace and war. Hence, without overall support from the public for a decisive political enterprise, it will not be possible to stop the dangerous downhill slide on the slope of the "peace process."

The self-deception that undermines the nation's instinct for survival is the result of continuous brainwashing, media distraction, cynical exploitation of accumulated weariness, and economic abundance that emasculates willpower. To restore the Israeli public to rationality, a systematic, constant, and comprehensive information campaign is necessary.

A harsh reality emerges from the above document, a result anticipated from political defeatism. However, Israel has the physical and mental potential to halt the grave developments described above, and to restore the Jewish state to the path of security and prosperity.

However, the question is not what can be done, but whether there is enough of a survival instinct left in Israel to abandon the "peace process" and pay the heavy price of shattering expectations.

There is not one incident in the history of humanity
in which defeatism led to peace
which was anything other than a complete fraud.

Douglas MacArthur

This Chapter was written in 2000, but no macro trends in the Middle East
have been changed since it was published; on the contrary, certain trends
have even been emphasized.

The Striking Similarity in Palestinian and Nazi Racism

Itamar Marcus, *Director, Palestinian Media Watch*

FOR MORE THAN fifty years, state-promoted genocide had been taboo. Although, there have been national leaders since the defeat of Nazi Germany who have orchestrated mass murder, no government has openly preached genocide as a systematic ideology of public policy. This taboo has been broken now by the Palestinian Authority.

Prior to World War II, the Nazis prepared the German people to commit the horrors of the Holocaust through a systematic indoctrination, demonizing Jews and Judaism, incorporating three fundamental principles:

1 that Jews are inferior, even sub-human;
2 that Jews are planning and executing heinous crimes which constitute a mortal danger, if unchecked;
3 defensive action is necessary for protection against the Jewish threat.

The systematic murder of Jews was transformed in Nazi ideology from a vicious atrocity to an act of idealism, which would save their people and the world.

Although, no evil in history is comparable to the Holocaust, it is now clear that the Palestinian Authority [PA] leadership is communicating a political-religious ideology that promotes genocide of the Jewish People, with haunting echoes of these three principles of Nazi ideology. The Jew's inferiority is reflected in the repeated dehumanization of Jews including cartoons depicting them as rats, worms, scorpions, spiders and octopuses.

A religious leader on official PA television defined the Jews: "...Allah's enemies, the nation accursed in the Qur'an, whom the Creator refers to as monkeys and pigs, calf-worshippers and idolaters... The Qur'an is plain... the worst enemies of the Islamic Nation are the Jews ..."[1]

Jews are portrayed as corrupt, deceitful, unfaithful, and especially, the cursed enemies of Allah. The political cartoon in the official Palestinian daily [Al Hayat Al Jadida], days before the end of the last millenium, defined the Jew as "the disease of the century."[2]

The second component of Palestinian indoctrination accuses the Jews of heinous crimes and posing a mortal threat, if not stopped.

• These libelous accusations drew considerable world attention when Suha Arafat stood beside Hillary Clinton and accused Israel of using poisonous gas.

• Other examples of PA fabricated accusations include: dropping poisoned candy from helicopters into Palestinian schoolyards[3]; distributing carcinogenic food[4]; injecting the AIDS virus into Arab prisoners; marketing radioactive belts to Arabs[5]; engaging in physical and mental torture of Palestinians; and sexually exploiting Arab children.

Once a population is convinced of the Jews' inferiority, lethal danger, and the enmity of God towards Jews, it is only a small step to seek out self-defense through the extermination of that evil threat. This is the most dangerous component.

• A member of the Palestinian Council of Religious Edicts, spelled it out on PA TV: "Jews are Jews. Whether Labor [Party] or Likud [Party]. Jews are Jews... [One] must slaughter them and kill them, as per the word of Allah... Do not have mercy in your hearts for Jews anywhere, in any country. Fight them wherever you are.

---

1   Sheikh Dr. Ibrahim Muhammad Maadi, Friday Sermon, PA TV, August 3, 2000
2   Al Hayat Al Jadida, Dec. 28, 1999
3   Al Hayat Al Jadida, Mar. 22 2001
4   Al-Hayat Al-Jadida, Sept. 12, 1998
5   Al Hayat Al Jadida, May 8, 2001

Anywhere you meet them – kill them. Kill the Jews... Do not have mercy on the Jews. Kill them everywhere."[6]

• Just last month a PA religious leader explained the inherently evil nature of the Jew, since the days of Muhammad:

"The Prophet Muhammad, whom the Jews tried to assassinate more than once, with poison and by witchcraft ...warned us of the Jews, of the Jews' evil and the Jews' deceit. He [Muhammad] battled them and expelled them from Arabia, saying: 'There shall not be two religions in Arabia.' And he clarified the character of the Jew in the Qur'an and in the sayings of the Prophet, so we would beware of them at every moment and at all times, and so that we would know how to deal with the Jews. Say to the Jews:... 'Expect your graveyard. Expect the final battle.'[7]

The obligation to kill Jews is presented not only as a religious precept, but has been cited repeatedly as a historical necessity – a precondition set by Allah anticipating the Islamic Day of Resurrection. As a senior religious leader, responsible for religious education in the Waqf, writing in Arafat's official daily, explained:

"The battle with the Jews will continue, because the Prophet has decreed it, and none of his words go unfulfilled.... [as the *Hadith* (Muslim oral tradition) states:] 'The Day of Resurrection will not come until the Muslims make war against the Jews and kill them, and until the Jew hides behind a rock and tree, and the rock and tree says: 'Oh Muslim, servant of Allah, a Jew is behind me, come and kill him!'...'[8]

Indeed, Allah's war against the Jews is predetermined and cannot be avoided, even through a future peace agreement: "... the nation of Palestine, our destiny from Allah is to be the vanguard in the war against the Jews... all the agreements are temporary...'[9]

The earmarking of the Jews as worthy of death from Allah is taught

---

6 Dr. Ahmad Yussouf Abu-Halabiyeh, PA TV Oct. 13, 2000
7 Mustafa Nadjem PA TV Feb 8, 2002
8 Sheikh Muhammed Abd Al Hadi La'afi, Al-Hayat Al-Jadida, May 18, 2001, also on PA TV Mar. 30, 2001, Apr. 13, 2001, Apr. 27, 2001, and Aug. 3, 2001, and others.
9 Dr. Ahmad Yussouf Abu-Halabiyeh, Palestinian Council of Religious Edicts, PA TV, July 28, 2000.

even in the new schoolbooks written in 2001 by the PA Education Ministry, which include passages from the Qur'an, teaching that Jews should long for death, from Allah himself.[10]

History keeps reminding us, as it tragically did on September 11, that evil ideology, if unchecked, will lead to heinous crimes against humanity. It was a common error prior to World War 11 for people to minimize Nazi hatred, dismissing it as rhetoric or propaganda. Tens of millions of people paid with their lives because the world couldn't bring itself to believe that there existed a nation that would put state murder into practice.

In explaining the civilized world's inability to recognize the danger of Nazism, Justice Robert H. Jackson, Chief US Counsel to the Nuremberg Trials, wrote:

"We must not forget that when the Nazi plans were boldly proclaimed, they were so extravagant that the world refused to take them seriously."[11]

Now it is the Palestinians who boldly and extravagantly proclaim their plans. Let us not make the same mistake again.

---

10 "... Jews, if you think that you are favored of Allah, to the exclusion of (other) men. Then long for death if you are truthful... death from which you flee, will surely overtake you. Reading the Qur'an, 6th grade PA school book, p.23.

11 *"Trial of War Criminal (Washington 1945) Indictment of Nazi Individuals and Organizations by the International Military Tribunal"*, p. 1138, US State Department publication

A Palestinian State: Clear and Immediate Danger to Inter-Arab Relations

David Bukay, *Political Science Department, The University of Haifa*

A PALESTINIAN STATE, if established, would probably exist in one of two forms, both of which embody an acute danger to the regional Arab and even the international surroundings: the first type, is a PLO state on the pattern of Arafat leadership, and the other is a fundamental Islamic state on the pattern of Hamas or *Jihad* Islamic leadership. We will not discuss here a Palestinian state under the leadership of local personalities, like Sari Nusseibah, not because this is not desirable, but because of the very low probability to its rise and the poor prospects to its long existence. We will consider the hazards of a Palestinian state to inter-Arab relations under two working conditions: first, the Palestinian independent state will be circumscribed in the territorial boundaries of 1967; second, the Kingdom of Jordan and the State of Israel will continue to exist and be located east and west of the Palestinian state, respectively. Any change in these two conditions would probably alter the terms and circumstances dealt with in this research.

To understand why we think a Palestinian state will threaten and jeopardize the Arab system, we need to analyze its main characteristics. Inter-Arab relations are characterized by common interactions on two continuities, which are pulling in two different directions: the first continuity is between cooperation to conflict, symbolized by a mixed-motives game, but with clear inclination towards the conflict pole, and the second continuity is between change to balancing, symbolized as a balance of power system, but with clear inclination towards the balancing pole.

Unique to the Arab system, there is a clear-cut distinction between two types of foreign policy: the first, the *watani* type, is the patriotic-statehood foreign policy, which is closely related and intertwined with the interests of the specific Arab state; the second, the *qawmi* type, which is closely related to Arab unity components and principles and strives for the abolition of the boundaries of the territorial states. Between these two types there exists an essential contradiction, and excluding few irregularities, the balancing considerations of the *watani* type have always prevailed. Despite this, the *qawmi* type of foreign policy has never disappeared, and it has a considerable and direct knot within Arab politics. The Arab states cannot, even if they wanted to, withdraw from it, and it obliges and compels them to work together in the name of, and for values for which they have no trust or even consent. Under these circumstances, they pay only lip service to the *qawmi* values, and declare only half-heartedly that they strive to achieve its goals.

The two most important motives of the *qawmi* type are: "Arab unity" and "Arab commitment to the solution of the Palestinian issue." These two are closely related, since only by the liberation of Arab land from "Zionist occupation" can the Arab states fulfill their glorious goals and achieve Arab unity. Under these circumstances and conditions one can understand the Arab involvement and intervention in Palestine. The long-range result is that they preferred all-Arab activities to realistic considerations of national interest. The Palestinian issue emphasized the Arab weakness and projected the lack of Arab unity. Israel has become a mirror in which the Arabs analyzed and examined their political and actual weaknesses. The Palestinian leadership exploited and utilized this Arab shame, the injuries to Arab honor, to deepen and exacerbate pan-Arab involvement and intervention in the Arab-Israeli conflict.

The Arab states, by and large, got involved and intervened in Palestine under false and erronious considerations. Some of the states were even dragged in, in contradiction to their best interests. But no less difficult a problem will be their effort not to be dragged in again to the long-standing inter-Arab confrontations, and not to be involved against their will in military activities with Israel. These conditions would even worsen if an independent Palestinian state were to be established. One can understand these trends better when they are analyzed according to the Réal-Politique School in international relations, with the focus on the balance of power between states in international relations. The state is the key actor striving to establish and maintain national interests in power terms and by maximizing its national security. Each system is divided among big-powers, middle-sized powers and small states. The small states are vital since they enable systemic flexibility. Yet, the big-powers of the system have to make sure that the small states will not disturb its functioning and will not drag it to imbalances, confrontations and wars.

Our main argument is that, under the circumstances prevailing in Palestinian society and leadership; their declared targets; the human problems of their Diaspora; and its existence between Jordan and Israel, with both serving as historic territories of Palestine, there are high prospects that the Palestinian state will be violent, irredentist, terrorist, unstable internally, and that it will externalize its internal problems. This Palestinian state will become a severe regional issue that will exacerbate the stability and intensify the war risks. What the Palestinian Authority exhibits now will be as naught compared to the situation that might be created.

BALANCE OF POWER THEORIES aim at the achievement and maintenance of political stability and the prevention of the eruption of crises and wars. The inter-Arab system is a typical balance of power system, with big-powers and small states, and it functions to establish balance and hegemony prevention. But a Palestinian state would bring back the ideological and political rivalries and disrupt stability, since, by its nature and objectives, it will turn to the radical and extremist states in the region to get patronage, defense and assistance. An "Arab cold war" will soon erupt again, as in Egypt during the Nasser era, and this situation may become an "Arab hot war," as in the Yemen war in the 1960s. If the Palestinian state would be Islamic in its nature, it could present a threat, if only by its success, to its neighbors – Jordan, Egypt, and even

Syria. Inter-Arab relations, which have become, from the second half of the 1980s, stable, even moderate, while discarding the utopian and unrealistic ideologies about Arab unity and the dissolution of the Arab states, might enter again a violent and conflictual era, and get involved deeply and directly once more in the "Arab commitment to the solution of the Palestinian issue."

COALITION THEORIES are most important in political systems and aim to assure and accelerate the power of its parties. A Palestinian state would create a polar inter-Arab system between coalitions of states that will focus on regional issues and leadership rivalries for power and domination, and hence will prevent concentration on the real domestic issues. A Palestinian state would create immediate coalitions with the most radical states in the Arab area – Iraq, Iran and Libya – and the inter-Arab rivalry might intensify and become exacerbated once again through the re-crystallization of ideological camps, such as the consent-front and the refusal-front of the 1970s. And if the Palestinian state would be Islamic in its nature, the immediate coalition would be with Iran, Sudan, and Somalia, no less than with other extremist fundamentalist factors. The result would be structurally and ideologically opposed coalitions seeking a common denominator in the total struggle against Israel, and relying on rival Arab states.

ARMS RACE THEORIES suggest that an arms race in a conflictual system with high tension is inclined to undermine and harm political stability, and create crises and wars. A Palestinian state will externalize its national independence, as a result of unrealized domestic pressures, and hence will accelerate the arms race in the region. There should be no illusion: no one can stop the arming of a Palestinian state, even by signed treaties, and the situation today proves this quite well. Jordan and Israel will do their best to balance these threats, but an arms race will take shape in regional dimension – with the participation of other actors. Instead of calm and moderation and focusing on acute internal needs, there will be a diversion to activist and violent foreign policy aimed especially against Israel. We may take an analogy from Egypt in the mid-1950s, when Nasser realized that there would be no great internal success, and that in order to keep his power, he must externalize his policy. In the foreign policy arena he could achieve status, prestige and political support without having to pay a price. Arafat's travels all around the world demonstrate the point. In his political career, he never paid attention to the Palestinian population's welfare, education, health and employment. From his point of view, there is only one destiny he must fulfill – the complete liberation of Palestine. The Palestinian political system, in its PLO or Islamic version, will act accordingly, out of necessity. It will turn to the international system and link itself to all radical and extreme forces with the aim of reaching its goals. Since Arafat entered Gaza, in July 1994, the Palestinian Authority has received billions of dollars, and yet one cannot find even one refugee family salvaged from the camps. The purchase of modern weapons, the acquisition of heavy armaments, and hence a considerable and risky arms race, will be the symbol of Palestinian independence, which may push the Middle East to new levels of violence and instability.

DETERRENCE THEORIES attempt to prevent the opponent from acting militarily, persuading him by means of cost–benefit behavior. Deterrence is a politics of assurances and threats and has close links to mutual perceptions and images. The aim of deterrence is to influence the opponent's way of thinking, and to shape his moves. But, when one speaks of a Palestinian state, in the PLO or Islamic version, the supposition that it will act rationally and with due care and caution is illusory. This is a terror and violence system, nihilistic in its thinking and activity, and, in the Islamic case, wishes to reject the past as well as the future. This situation is exacerbated when one recalls that in the Middle East, patrimonial leadership and authoritarian political systems are the rule. There is no citizenship, no political opinion, no interest groups, and certainly no political freedoms. Everything stems from the leader's wishes, perceptions and activities. He works alone and his word is law. Hence the supposition that the population's needs will moderate his leadership is quite unrealistic. He who hesitates to come to this conclusion, to reach out to this insight, would do well to analyze the circumstances from which Arafat launched the terrorist era in September 2000 in the territories. Arafat is a serial terrorist, a total liar, whose métier is killing and destruction. He has no moral restraints and no political impediments to achieving his aims. He did not hesitate to fight in Jordan in 1970 and to bring about civil war; he did not refrain from fighting against Syria and the Lebanese in Lebanon and to bring death and destruction to Beirut; and he did not hesitate to harm and damage the Palestinian way of life, to establish a corrupt system and send hundreds of Palestinians to their death. We have every reason to believe that even deterrence by the big powers of the region is unlikely to succeed in preventing violent activities of the Palestinian state, and the purchase of armaments in huge amounts that will continue to disrupt the region's balance of power.

RATIONALITY OF POLITICAL SYSTEMS THEORIES is an outcome of cultural dimensions. Indeed, in most cases, states behave rationally. The problem is that what seems clearly rational in one place or situation, hardly seems the same in another place or situation. The values, the perceptions, and the subjective tendencies dictate a behavior and activity that are grasped differently. Although there are cases in which states lose balance and reasonability considerations, and hence drag themselves to unaccountable activity, in most cases they act in a calculated policy. Yet, the proposition of the rationality of the Palestinian state is basically founded on "the image mirror," and it is in the eye of the beholder. From its activity point of view, and especially its *raison d'Etat*, this is not necessarily the interest of the Palestinian state. We have proofs that its rational target will be to undermine and disrupt regional stability, because its political and economical existence is at stake, when it is circumscribed between Jordan and Israel, which both have large Palestinian populations. (In Jordan the Palestinian population constitutes a majority). Those who think that this is a recipe for regional stability are cordially invited to analyze many historical situations in Europe in the past, and in Asia and Africa today. There is every reason for apprehension that a Palestinian state, in these circumstances, and with this point of departure, will violate all international norms, and that in the future the international community will be faced with a situation similar to that of Iraq under Saddam Hussein, or of Al Qaida in Afghanistan.

The international community agreed, after generations of bloody wars, on acceptable norms and patterns of behavior, but we have good reason to fear that a Palestinian state will become an unresolved issue in the inter-Arab political agenda. One has to analyze the political ripeness issue. The critical question is whether the Palestinian leadership is mature enough to accept national responsibility and to act moderately and cautiously. Its crystallization may raise deep gaps between the political aspirations of the leadership and what can be achieved. The result will be frustrations and disappointments that will lead to violent aggression. The situation among the Palestinian refugees will worsen, becoming an unsettling factor for the continuation of violent struggle and terrorism. The political system in the Middle East is liable to enter again the dark eras of political rivalries and even wars.

What is to be done from an inter-Arab point of view? The aim should be, as a moderate policy, to establish a protectorate state for the Palestinians that will be administered by a group of mandatory democratic states from the international system, and representatives from the Arab states, with observers from Israel and Jordan. This mandatory management will be supervised and inspected by the international powers, and the declared goal is to bring the Palestinian population to political maturity and national responsibility as a long-range policy. The international management will be especially focused on the economic and educational fields, so as to create a viable and non-violent society, a moderate and not a suicidal-murderous society; and to establish a responsible leadership ready to help Palestinians achieve limited aspirations, and to accept the regional circumstances without disrupting and undermining the existing political situation. In any event, every crucial change in the political situation of the protectorate state will require the consent of Jordan and Israel.

To those who will argue that the mandatory era ended long ago and that it is anachronistic, the answer will be that the possibility of a violent terrorist state endangering the existence of other states and violating the regional stability, such as the Palestinian state represents, must be counteracted. To those who "care" for the right of self-determination for the Palestinians, one should say that the alternative is acute regional wars, and the continuation of crises and tensions. There are many minorities in the world who seek to have national independence, and one does not hear voices for their right of self-determination. On the inter-Arab political system of the Middle East, the suggested policy of protectorate might gain a political consensus, until the circumstances will change crucially among the Palestinians themselves.

Impact on American Interests

Michael Widlanski

SHOULD AMERICA and the West support the establishment of a Palestinian state in the West Bank and Gaza?

The answer to that question depends mainly on the answer to another question:

Will the establishment of a Palestinian state help or hinder American interests?

There are many ways to describe American interests in strategic, tactical, historical, moral or economic terms: opposing dictatorship, supporting democracy, supporting free markets etc. However the best short-hand guide is offered by history.

Throughout the twentieth century and now at the beginning of the twenty-first, America's role in the world parallels the role of Great Britain in an earlier era: a global trading power interested primarily in stability for the sake of business.

Does establishing a Palestinian state help or hinder regional stability and global stability?

If history is any guide, the prospects are not optimistic.

Yasser Arafat's Palestine Liberation Organization has had three near-state experiences: Jordan, 1969–70; Lebanon, 1976–82; and Gaza/West Bank 1994–2002.

In each of the cases, countries adjacent to the PLO base-state felt waves of instability, resulting in war.

Nevertheless, some American policy makers believe that backing a Palestinian state gives America increased clout in the Arab world, including access to Arab oil. The Arab states want a Palestinian state, and opposing this desire puts America at odds with the powerful Arab world. Further, it is argued that respecting the right of self-determination requires America and the West to push for a Palestinian Arab state.

Let us look at these arguments.

ARAB STATES AND A PALESTINIAN STATE

The question of a Palestinian state is a classic example of how in the Arab political community there is often a wide gulf between a public pronouncement and the real political position.

From the time of the United Nations partition of the British Mandatory territory of Palestine, the Arab world has spoken boldly about Palestinian rights – such as self-determination – but acted in quite a different manner.

The Arab armies that invaded Israel/Palestine did so at the behest of Arab leaders who had no intention of building a Palestinian national state, but only in furthering their own stature and enlarging their own territorial holdings.

The Hashemite Kingdom of Transjordan (later Jordan) absorbed Palestinian territory – Judea and Samaria (West Bank) and parts of Jerusalem. Transjordan changed its name but did not offer Palestinian Arabs their own state during the transition. There is no question that the Hashemite family, despite its public statements, views another Arab state as a destabilizing element. By furthering such a state, America and its Western allies would actually be undermining Jordan, one of the most benign Arab states.

Egypt, which for years pretended to be the protector of the Palestinians, actually penned the Palestinian refugees inside horrible refugee camps. Egypt's president Gamal Abdul-Nasser exploited the refugees and the Palestinian Question (Arabic: Al-Qadiyya Al-Felastiniyya) to promote his own career as a pan-Arab leader. The hapless Palestinians inside the Egyptian-controlled Gaza Strip were not even offered Egyptian citizenship.

Abdul-Nasser's successor, Anwar Sadat, made a Middle Eastern peace possible by moving away from the pan-Arab approach of Abdul-Nasser. While Sadat publicly called for Palestinian statehood, he was willing to accept "Palestinian autonomy."

The current Egyptian president Husni Mubarrak has moved back in the direction of Abdul-Nasser, again using the Palestinian card as a source for legitimization of Egypt as leader of the Arab world. But there are signs that forces unleashed inside the Palestinian Authority threaten Egypt as well as Israel – such as Intifada rioting and Islamic fanaticism.

Syria, which also absorbed Palestinian refugees after 1948, has consistently opposed an independent Palestinian state. The ruling Ba'ath Party of Syria regards Palestine as part of Greater Syria (Arabic: Al-Suriyya Al-Kubra). Syria has occasionally supported the PLO as a pawn in power struggles with and inside its neighbors (e.g. Jordan, 1970), but it has also directly attacked the PLO on many occasions and even tried to assassinate PLO leader Arafat (e.g. in northern Lebanon, 1983).

Saudi Arabia, which has sent much financial aid to the PLO, seems to do so as a form of "protection racket" – buying insurance against Palestinian-fomented insurgency. The Saudi-led Arab oil embargo of 1973 had little to do with Arab political demands and everything to do with enlarging oil revenues. Indeed, of the huge oil revenues netted by the Saudi princes, only a microscopic speck ends up in the hands of the average Palestinian. Documents captured in 2001 by the Israeli Police in Orient House (a PLO forward base in Jerusalem) as well as by the Israeli Army in 2002 at Arafat's Ramallah headquarters show that much Saudi aid has been siphoned off by the corrupt Palestinian leadership rather than going to fix sewage in Gaza or hospitals in the West Bank.

Actions speak louder than words. During the three principal Israeli-Palestinian clashes (1982 War in Lebanon, 1987–89 Intifada and the current Palestinian-Israeli War of Atrrition), the Arab world has largely sat on the sidelines.

In short, the four immediate Arab neighbors of a potential Palestine have not spent any real efforts to build a Palestinian Arab state, and they are not likely to expend political capital on this matter in the future.

More distant Arab states such as Libya and Iraq have been more forthright in their support of the PLO and a Palestinian state, but they are not likely to give up their weapons of mass destruction or terroristic intentions in exchange for American support for a Palestinian state.

ISRAEL AND A PALESTINIAN STATE

Israel is America's most valuable and most stable ally in the Middle East, and it is directly threatened by the establishment of a Palestinian Arab state.

American presidents from Harry Truman to George W. Bush have seen a special tie to Israel based on three major themes:
- Historic ties;
- Moral ties;
- And Strategic ties.

A Jewish State that rose out of the ashes of the Holocaust was seen as a moral imperative by Truman and Eisenhower (who visited the death camps).

Truman overruled the narrow perspective of his own Department of State and recognized Israel because of this moral imperative and because of the democratic values of the new state – the only "Third World" state that came into being after World War II that has had an uninterrupted democratic existence.

Subsequently, American presidents came to respect Israel for its battlefield mettle and strategic value (even Eisenhower, whose administration approved military aid to Israel in the late part of his second term).

John Kennedy, Lyndon Johnson, Richard Nixon and Ronald Reagan saw Israel as a prime strategic asset in the global battle against Communism. They correctly saw Israel as a tremendous intelligence asset and as a bastion of democratic stability inside the roiling Mediterranean basin. The American Bicentennial saw this element symbolically demonstrated by the fantastically successful Israeli rescue operation to free plane passengers hijacked to Entebbe, Uganda by Arab hijackers.

There have been many such bold Israeli actions over the years, though not all have become public.

Indeed, there were often cases when American presidents scolded

Israel for her military boldness – only to admit later that she was right. The bold Israeli demolition of Iraq's nuclear option (then) in 1981 is a prime example.

With the fall of Communism, however, some of the "pro-Arab" voices in the Department of State grew strong again. They claimed that Israel's value as a strategic asset had diminished if not disappeared entirely.

This short-sighted view should have been shelved after the first attack on the World Trade Center in New York in 1993 at the behest of Islamic terrorists. The specter of Pan-Islamic and Pan-Arab terror has reared its head on many other occasions over the last 12 years, even though there were many Western policy makers who preferred not to pay attention.

More than a year after the major attacks on the United States of September 2001, there are voices who minimize this threat and who simultaneously speak of "leashing" Israel. These voices should not be heeded.

In short, the strategic value of Israel to the West – and to America in particular – is greater than ever before, and the moral and historical ties between Israel and the US are as strong as ever.

But establishing a Palestinian Arab state endangers Israel, America's top ally in the region.

HOW PALESTINE THREATENS ISRAEL
Opponents of a Palestinian state argued for years that it would become a terrorist base operating against Israel. Terrorists operating from inside the Gaza Strip or West Bank could easily reach Israeli cities, they said.

They further argued that such a state would become an outpost for Communist or other extreme movements (such as Islamic radicalism).

Opponents of a Palestinian state said that Israel's own Arab population would be radicalized and turned against its own government and the Jewish majority.

This is only a short list of the threats, but all the items on the list have already been realized.

Proponents of a Palestinian state argued that such a state could be demilitarized and democratic, but it has not worked out that way.

In fact, the current Palestinian leadership has set back movement toward "Palestinian Civil Society" by many years.

It is not within the scope of this article to address detailed political solutions. However, it will have succeeded if it has convinced the reader that establishing a Palestinian Arab state under present circumstances is worse than a dead-end street. It is an open invitation to disaster.

Michael Widlanski, former Middle East Bureau Chief for the Cox Newspapers and a former reporter for The New York Times, teaches at the Rothberg School of Hebrew University.

Part II

ALTERNATIVE SOLUTIONS

THEN: Palestine
NOW: Jordan and Israel

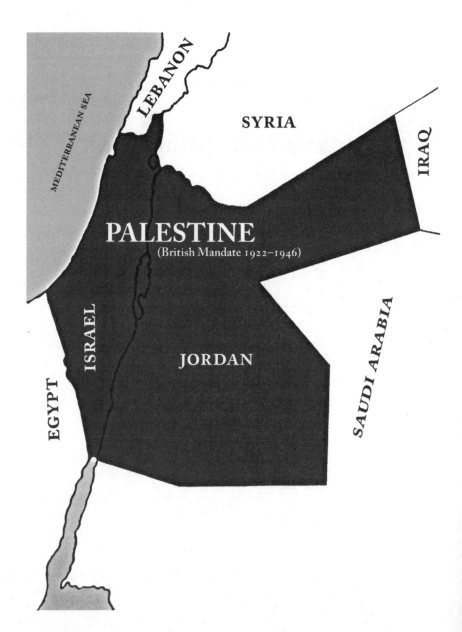

Palestine in Middle East Peace

The late Paul S. Riebenfeld, *Columbia University, New York,*
submitted this statement before the United States Congress
subcommittee hearing.

A T THE PRESENT STAGE of trying to sort out the complexities of the Middle East conflict, the terms in which the Palestinian question is being debated has become a principle obstacle on the road to peace. The exigencies of belligerency and mass agitation in the Arab countries and among their allies in the Third World have succeeded in distorting the political, geographical and demographic elements on which any peace settlement has to be based, in a manner which makes such a settlement practically impossible to attain. There is no way of dealing with the Palestinian issue constructively, unless the terms "Palestine" and "Palestinians" are defined correctly instead of being manipulated as functions of a policy geared to guerrilla warfare, "revolutionary upheaval," and "wars of national liberation."

Opinion on the Palestinian question is greatly affected by an understanding of what is meant by "Palestine." Due to the power of one-sided propaganda the terms "Palestine" and "Palestinians" have become subject to manipulation in accordance with the shifts of short-term political expediency – as though one were dealing with a country arbitrarily carved out of nowhere. Palestine, in fact, has boundaries which for centuries were recorded and imprinted upon the memory of mankind. Even when it had disappeared from the political map and was treated for centuries as part of Syria, its geography was well-known. When its political identity was restored at the end of World War I with the Palestine Mandate, its legal boundaries were laid down accordingly.

Until the demise of the League of Nations, in 1946, the Palestine Mandate, as granted to Great Britain at the San Remo Conference of 1920 and confirmed by the League in 1922, covered a territory of 45,820 square miles east and west of the Jordan. Its boundaries reached from the Mediterranean in the West until Iraq in the East. Thus all of Jordan was encompassed within the borders of Palestine.

Trans-Jordan was in fact what the relevant League of Nations file calls "the Trans-Jordan Province" of Palestine until the final winding-up meeting of the League of Nations, on April 18, 1946. The often expressed opinion that Trans-Jordan was excluded from the Palestine Mandate in 1922 is not correct.

At present the very terminology of the discussion of the Palestine issue has been dictated by a skilful agitation which has made at first journalists and then also diplomats call "Palestinians" those Arabs who are refugees or children of refugees from what is now Israel, or Arab inhabitants of the "West Bank" and the Gaza strip. Neither history nor international law justify that usage. Historically and legally, the term "Palestine" can only mean the full territory included in the Palestine Mandate after World War I – what is now Israel and Jordan and the lands in dispute between them. The word "Palestine" had no clear-cut geographical denotation and represented no political identity before the First World War. "Palestinians" are therefore all people – Jews and Arabs – who live in or have the right to live in the territory of the Palestine Mandate as constituted in 1920, confirmed by the League of Nations in 1922, and unchanged during the lifetime of the League of Nations until 1946. Both Jordan and Israel have emerged as successor states of the Palestine Mandate, on its territory east and west of the Jordan: a Palestinian Arab state and a Palestinian Jewish state, "successors" to the sovereignty of Turkey via the League of Nations.

International law and history do not always decide policy, but they are indispensable for an understanding of issues. They form the broad background of the day-to-day diplomacy of states. It should not be impossible to explain even to the peoples, governments and intellectuals of Third World countries that the acceptance of the Jewish state idea by the international order has been an organic part of the movement toward national self-determination that has resulted in the establishment of twenty Arab states so far and one Jewish state.

That there does not exist an Arab state called "Palestine" is not the responsibility of Zionism or of Israel. Nor is it, after all, a matter of substance, since the greater part of Palestine is Arab-governed and inhabited by Palestinian Arabs. As a matter of fact, since the ending of the British Palestine Mandate it has been a purely internal Arab matter, depending mainly on the relationship between the Arab people of Palestine and the Hashemite dynasty ruling Jordan. It is, however, an unassailable fact that at least 85 percent of the Arab people of Palestine are living still today in the area of the former Palestine Mandate.

The advocacy of the Palestinian cause, as formulated in its conclaves in Cairo, Algiers or Rabat, has been aimed, in short, at maintaining the thrust against Israel, rather than recognizing, Jordan as the Palestinian Arab nation-state that it truly is. Both its land and its people are Palestinian. So is King Hussein.

In his memoirs, Hussein had written: "Palestine and Jordan were both (by then) under British Mandate, but as my grandfather pointed out in his memoirs, they were hardly separate countries. Trans-Jordan being to the east of the river Jordan, it formed, in a sense, the interior of Palestine."

Yasser Arafat, while the issue of "Palestinian Arab self-determination" was first debated at the United Nations, when asked what he thought about a West Bank state, [said] to Eric Roleau: "The watchdogs of the counter-revolution have become very busy since we have been confronting serious difficulties, but those fishing in troubled waters will not succeed in dividing our people, which extends to both sides of the Jordan, in spite of the artificial boundaries established by the Colonial Office and Winston Churchill half a century ago."

While still in Jordan, Arafat had told Oriana Fallaci that the PLO was fighting Israel in the name of pan-Arabism. He added: "What you call Trans-Jordan is actually Palestine." This view, although in contradiction to the claim that the destruction of the State of Israel can satisfy the claim for Palestinian Arab self-determination, has not been changed. The very day Arafat left Cairo for New York to address the UN General Assembly, he sent (according to Al Liwa, Beirut) a message to a student conference held in Baghdad, that contained the sentence: "Jordan as well as Palestine is ours, we shall establish our national entity on both territories once they are liberated from Israeli occupation and Jordanian reactionary presence." While public attention has been riveted on the PLO challenge to Israel, especially after the decision of the Rabat conference to nominate the PLO the sole representative of the Arab people of Palestine, the challenge remains greater to King Hussein's* rule of Jordan.

The London Economist spoke of a Jordanian General Election as a "time-bomb" ticking away. "More than half the voters would be Palestinians – but should they vote for a Jordanian government when they are supposed to be represented by the Palestinian Liberation Organization? On the other hand can the majority be disenfranchised?" How much better Hussein* would be off if he had been induced to abandon his pose as a benevolent "host" to "refugees" and to affirm the fact that Jordan is the Palestinian Arab nation-state just as Israel is the Palestinian Jewish nation-state.

What exactly happened on September 16, 1922, the date that has played a considerable role in the Palestine debate for decades? It has distorted the vision and knowledge of otherwise informed and conscientious writers and politicians. And, curiously, the perspective has been warped more among Israeli and Western scholars than among the Arabs.

In vain will the diplomat or scholar look in the files of the League of Nations or any other archives for evidence that in the year 1922, or any other year before 1946, took place the "severance" or "separation" of Trans-Jordan from Palestine; the "Partition" of Palestine; the establishment of a "Mandate of Trans-Jordan"; or "Trans-Jordan Independence" or any similar event with which the literature of the Middle East abounds.

---

* The same holds true for King Abdullah today.

Trans-Jordan remained a part of Palestine and the Palestine Mandate remained there in full force. What happened was that under an authorization contained in Article 25 of the Mandate, two months after confirmation of the Palestine Mandate by the League of Nations in July, 1922, the British government obtained the League's consent "to postpone or withhold" the application of the Jewish National Home provisions of the Mandate "in the territories lying between the Jordan and the eastern boundary of Palestine." Article 25 of the Palestine Mandate reads in full: "In the territories lying between the Jordan and the eastern boundary of Palestine as ultimately determined, the Mandatory shall be entitled, with the consent of the Council of the League of Nations, to postpone or withhold application of such provisions of the mandate as he may consider inapplicable to the existing local conditions, and to make such provision for the administration of the territories as he may consider suitable to those conditions, provided that no action shall be taken which is inconsistent with the provisions of Articles 15, 16 and 18." In what the relevant file of the League of Nations describes as the "Trans-Jordan Province" of Palestine, a local administration was established within the Palestine Mandate, headed by the Emir Abdullah, brother of King Faisal of Iraq. Zionist colonization was suspended in Trans-Jordan legally, though the suspension did not apply to individual Jewish settlement or even Jewish schools. But this did not mean that Trans-Jordan was legally separated from Palestine in any way as far as the Arab population of the country was concerned. There was no separate government; unlike the situation regarding Syria and Lebanon, which the mandatory was to develop into two separate states, Palestine was meant to remain one.

Trans-Jordan remained under the Palestine Mandate and was administered under the authority of the High Commissioner in Jerusalem. Trans-Jordanians traveled under his protection; under international law their nationality was Palestinian. Subject to safety requirements due to the character of the Bedouin majority in Trans-Jordan, Arabs moved freely between Cis- and Trans-Jordan; many Trans-Jordanian Palestine Arabs, either seasonally or permanently, settled and worked in places like Haifa, Jaffa or Jerusalem. The suspension of Zionist colonization in Trans-Jordan did not bring about its separation from Palestine but, in fact, secured its Palestinian Arab character.

Because of Zionist development and the constant clash between Arab and Jewish claims, accompanied by inquiry commissions, worldwide publicity, and parliamentary debates, public interest and controversy remained focused on Cis-Jordan. From 1922 on, with warrant in law, the habit grew of referring to Palestine only as that part of the mandate area associated with the Jewish National Home.

In 1937 the Palestine Royal Commission, reporting fairly on the underlying facts of the Arab-Jewish conflict, had agreed that Trans-Jordan was originally included in the Jewish National Home of the Palestine Mandate. The fact that Jewish development was suspended in that part of the country did not mean that the Arab-Jewish confrontation should not continue to be seen within the context of the large area of the whole of Palestine rather than the small area of Cis-Jordan. The Royal Commission included Trans-Jordan in its proposals for the future, and in its partition scheme joined it with the Arab parts of Cis-Jordan, even proposing a transfer of population between the planned Arab and Jewish states.

From a legal point of view there was never any doubt whatsoever about Trans-Jordan being a part of Palestine. Great Britain, in its attempts to appease Arab nationalism or to flatter the Emir Abdullah, may sometimes have allowed a degree of vagueness to be introduced into a speech or even an administrative document. The British were free, internally, to present their role in any way they wished. In international law, Trans-Jordan, administered by the Colonial Office, was subject to League of Nations supervision, and more particularly to the minute scrutiny of the Permanent Mandates Commission of the League of Nations. "Trans-Jordan" was quite an ordinary item among the headings of its annual agenda for Palestine; it was tucked in between, say "Public Health" and "Education."

Two examples are typical of the conscientiousness of the League Secretariat and the Mandate commission. In July 1926, almost four years after the passing of the Trans-Jordanian resolution of 1922, an internal League memorandum to the Secretary General raised the point that "from the strictly legal point of view this did not constitute a modification of the Mandate, but an application thereof" and inquired, since the Mandate document was to be put on sale, whether to call it "The Mandate for Palestine" or "The Mandate for Palestine and Trans-Jordan." The decision was for the title "Mandate for Palestine."

Even more decisive, from a legal point of view, was the discussion in the Council of the League of Nations in October 1928, on the agreement made in February of that year between Trans-Jordan and Great Britain, represented by the Palestine High Commissioner, which, the Mandate Commission reported to the Council, had raised doubts as to its compatibility with the Palestine Mandate. After a lengthy debate and an official declaration by the British delegate that "in Trans-Jordan the Palestine Mandate remain in full force" and that the administration of the Emir represents but a delegation of the administrative powers of the mandatory power, the Council of the League adopted the following resolution: "As regards the Agreement of February 20th, 1928, between Great Britain and Trans-Jordan, the Council takes note of the declaration of the representative of Great Britain according to which his Government regards itself as responsible to the League of Nations for the application in Trans-Jordan of the Palestine Mandate with the exception of the articles which, based on Article 25, are not applicable; and acknowledges that this agreement is in conformity with the principles of the mandate which remain in full force."

The efforts of the League of Nations, and in particular of the Permanent Mandates Commission, to maintain the integrity of Palestine as one country were based, in the main, on legal reasons, but also imbued by the consciousness of the special character of Palestine, and the political feeling that the Arab-Jewish confrontation required as wide a context as possible.

Eventually it was in connection with the United States opposition to the radically anti-Zionist policy adopted by the British Labour Government that its Foreign Minister Ernest Bevin decided, in the hiatus between the demise of the League of Nations and the inception of the United Nations, to remove Trans-Jordan altogether from the context of the Palestine problem, now coming under intensified scrutiny.

The Attlee-Bevin government, because of its negative response to President Truman's powerful appeal for the admission into Palestine of a limited number of Jewish survivors of the concentration camps, had good reason at the end of 1945 to fear a re-examination of the status of Trans-Jordan that would invalidate their contention that Palestine was too small a country to accommodate the number of Jewish survivors in Europe and that would put into question the long range strategic plans that the Foreign Office had for the future of Palestine and for the role of General Glubb's Arab Legion of Trans-Jordan. For, in November 1945, the Anglo-American Committee of Enquiry had been established. Beginning its sessions in December, it was scheduled to proceed in January to London, then to Europe, Cairo and Palestine.

Its terms of reference were to "examine political, economic and social conditions in Palestine as they bear upon the problem of Jewish immigration" and "to examine the position of the Jews in those countries in Europe where they have been the victims of Nazi and Fascist persecution" – terms of reference, in the words of the chairman of the Labour Party, "wide enough to make possible the abandonment of that administrative separation between Palestine and Trans-Jordan which was a grave initial error in British policy."

Mr. Bevin decided to avoid any risks; he took the bold step of announcing the forthcoming grant of independence to Trans-Jordan even while the Committee was about to begin its hearings in London, in the hope of dampening the commission's urge to extend its inquiry beyond Cis-Jordanian Palestine, as had been suggested in the Washington hearings.

It is an understatement to say that the step was of doubtful legality. "The Mandate does not make provisions for the Mandatory Power to concede mandatory power to the people under tutelage. That is a change of the Mandate," requiring consent of the League Council. There were specific rules, drawn up by the Permanent Mandates Commission and the League Council on the occasion of the ending of the Iraq Mandate in 1932, setting out the requirements which had to be examined before independence would be attained; and, most important of all, there were Articles 77 and 80 of the United Nations Charter specifying the applicability of the Trusteeship provisions to the existing Mandate territories and beyond doubt making it illegal in the meantime "to alter in any manner the rights whatsoever of any states or any people or the terms of existing international instruments..."

To this day Article 80 is colloquially referred to among international lawyers as the "Palestine Clause," because its insertion in the Charter at San Francisco was the result of work by Jewish representatives attempting to protect Jewish rights under the Mandate during the hiatus preceding activation of the United Nations organs. But the wording protected the rights of any people under Mandate administration.

The concluding session of the League of Nations in April 1946 in Geneva was presented by the British government with the giving of independence to a part of Palestine as a fait accompli, a matter of the past, and as though there had been a separate mandate for Trans-Jordan. The meeting took note of it.

The legal objections to independence could theoretically have come from the Secretariats of either the League of Nations or the United Nations. But they could also have come from the Jewish Agency, either based on its special legal status under the Mandate, which had not been cancelled by Article 25, or on Article 80 of the Charter. They could also have been made by a state on behalf of the Arabs or Jews of Palestine, under Article 80.

As it happened, the people whose interests were most neglected by the measures taken in 1946 were the Arabs of Cis-Jordan, today's "Palestinians." For the first time in history the Arabs of Western Palestine were cut off from the territory to the east of the Jordan. When less than two years later – following the example of their leaders and upper classes who had departed for Cairo, Beirut or Paris – masses of Palestinian Arabs abandoned their villages and streamed over the Jordan, they were considered legally no longer as Palestinians moving into another part of their homeland, but as foreign refugees received by a "host country." It was as though within the two years between May 1946 and May 1948 a new nation-state of Trans-Jordan had been born, with no links to Palestine or Palestinians.

Ever since, this distortion has affected political perception and

action in the Middle East. The simple acknowledgment that Jordan
is Arab Palestine would have been capable in the past, as it is capable
today, of changing the perspectives of the future.

Nothing can change the fact that the Hashemite Kingdom of Jordan is in reality the "Palestinian Kingdom of Hashemite Jordan." In this
role it could be the legitimate partner of Israel to achieve a settlement
of the Palestine conflict, which is the core of the Arab-Israeli conflict.
If instead it continues to divest itself of its Palestinian identity, even
its internal legitimacy will remain in jeopardy. The question is whether
King Hussein's undoubted physical courage denotes moral and political
courage of equal force, as well as a grasp of reality.

It is true that the acknowledged identity of Jordan as a Palestinian
country would give the lie to the overwrought version of the Arab-Israeli
conflict on which radical Arab propaganda and the success of the PLO
have been based. The myth of the "national homelessness" of the Arab
people would collapse and with it much of the popular passion it arouses
in Arab countries, exerting pressure on internal government policies.
However, those Arab leaders who have a sense of history and must wish
for the defusing of the bitterness of the conflict – if for no other reason
than the role Israel is playing in the overall strategic and technological
texture of the Middle East – might cooperate if a lead were given in
this direction, with the co-operation of the US Government.

Not only would the recognition that the whole territory of the
Hashemite Kingdom of Jordan is an integral part of Palestine, and of
the political and physical context of the Palestine issue, conform to the
facts of history, policy and law under the League of Nations Mandate,
it would create a realistic framework for the co-existence of Palestine
Arab and Jewish self-determination.

It should make a difference to the political and psychological
process of peace-making whether Israel is perceived as occupying 12
percent of the land area of Palestine since 1948, and a full 100 per cent
of the land area of Palestine since 1967, or whether it is realized that
it occupies 20 percent of the country to which the Palestine Mandate
applied, the remaining 80 percent of Palestine being still completely
Arab and Arab-governed.

It should make a difference to the legitimacy of King Hussein as representative leader of the Arab people of Palestine, whether such a role is based on the number of Cis-Jordanian Arabs in Trans-Jordan, or whether he is a Palestinian ruler by virtue of birth, of tradition, and of the political, legal and historical character of his country, to be expressed in its institutions.

It should make a difference to the prestige and the future of King Hussein, whether he affirms that the Hashemites, during the quarter of a century of the Mandate, succeeded in preserving four-fifths of Palestine as Arab, and based on this legitimacy, proceeds toward peace between Jordan as the Palestinian Arab nation-state and Israel as the Palestinian Jewish nation-state, or whether he will persist with the dubious concept of separate Jordanian and Palestinian identities, on which no local or regional stability can be built.

It should make a difference whether the Arab refugees and their children are told that in crossing the Jordan, in 1948, they entered a "host-country" or whether it is conceded that they entered that Arab part of their home country, which had recently acquired independence, gave them immediately their legitimate citizenship, and is entitled to their allegiance.

It should make a difference to Arab-Jewish reconciliation whether Israel's existence is conceived as resting on various faits accomplis, or resting on a fair and legitimate concept of rights inherent in the history of the region and in the legal structure of the Middle East since the First World War; whether the acceptance by the international order of the Jewish state idea has been an organic part of the movement toward national self-determination since the First World War, which has resulted so far in twenty Arab states and one Jewish state; or whether the establishment of Israel was merely the result of the international conscience being moved on account of the murder of a third of the Jewish people.

Stoking by such means the fires of popular passion, misrepresentation has escalated the Middle East conflict, and has added to its emotional dimensions immeasurably. By contributing to irrational pressures, the distortion of the Palestine problem acts as a powerful threat to the

Arab governments as much as it threatens peace-making. Willingness to defuse the emotional causes of the conflict may be the most important criterion for gauging the will to peace.

It is time that the Arab governments with a stake in stability and in the beginning of a peaceful era for the Middle East be encouraged to present a true picture of the development of the Palestine problem and a true definition of "Palestine" and "Palestinians." The ancient country, in its historical and geographical boundaries, can richly accommodate Jewish self-determination and Palestinian Arab self-determination.

Submitted for publication courtesy of Murray Greenfield

A Peace Plan

Menachem Begin

O N DECEMBER 28, 1977, Prime Minister Menachem Begin presented to the Knesset the Israeli plan for political autonomy for the residents of Gaza, Judea and Samaria. Begin discussed the plan at some length, and also raised the issue of proposed arrangements for returning the Sinai to Egypt. The debate on the plan lasted 12 hours, and was followed by a vote by the entire Knesset.

Following are the text of the peace plan presented by Prime Minister Begin, excerpts from his elaboration of the plan and his responses to the Knesset debate, and the result of the Knesset vote.

I. PRESENTATION OF THE 1977 PEACE PLAN

PRIME MINISTER MENACHEM BEGIN: Mr. Speaker, Members of the Knesset.

On the establishment of peace we shall propose to grant administrative self-rule to the Arab residents of Judea, Samaria and the Gaza District on the basis of the following:

ISRAEL'S PROPOSAL FOR PALESTINIAN AUTONOMY
Self-rule for Palestinian Arabs, Residents of Judea, Samaria, and the Gaza District, which will be instituted upon the establishment of peace:

1 The administration of the military government in Judea, Samaria and the Gaza District will be abolished.

2 In Judea, Samaria and the Gaza District, administrative autonomy of the residents, by and for them, will be established.

3 The residents of Judea, Samaria and the Gaza District will elect an Administrative Council composed of 11 members. The Administrative Council will operate in accordance with the principles laid down in this paper.

4 Any resident 18 years old or over, without distinction of citizenship, including stateless residents, is entitled to vote in the elections to the Administrative Council.

5 Any resident whose name is included in the list of candidates for the Administrative Council and who, on the day the list is submitted, is 25 years old or over, is eligible to be elected to the council.

6 The Administrative Council will be elected by general, direct, personal, equal, and secret ballot.

7 The period of office of the Administrative Council will be four years from the day of its election.

8 The Administrative Council will sit in Bethlehem.

9 All administrative affairs relating to the Arab residents of the areas of Judea, Samaria and the Gaza District will be under the direction and within the competence of the Administrative Council.

10 The Administrative Council will operate the following departments: education; religious affairs; finance; transportation; construction and housing; industry, commerce, and tourism; agriculture; health; labor and social welfare; rehabilitation of refugees; and the department for the administration of justice and the supervision of the local police forces. It will also promulgate regulations relating to the operation of these departments.

11 Security and public order in the areas of Judea, Samaria and the Gaza District will be the responsibility of the Israeli authorities.

12 The Administrative Council will elect its own chairman.

13 The first session of the Administrative Council will be convened 30 days after the publication of the election results.

14 Residents of Judea, Samaria and the Gaza District, without distinction of citizenship, including stateless residents, will be granted free choice of either Israeli or Jordanian citizenship.

15 A resident of the areas of Judea, Samaria and the Gaza District

who requests Israeli citizenship will be granted such citizenship in accordance with the citizenship law of the state.

16 Residents of Judea, Samaria and the Gaza District who, in accordance with the right of free option, choose Israeli citizenship, will be entitled to vote for, and be elected to, the Knesset in accordance with the election law.

17 Residents of Judea, Samaria and the Gaza District who are citizens of Jordan or who, in accordance with the right of free option, become citizens of Jordan, will elect and be eligible for election to the Parliament of the Hashemite Kingdom of Jordan in accordance with the election law of that country.

18 Questions arising from the vote to the Jordanian Parliament by residents of Judea, Samaria and the Gaza District will be clarified in negotiations between Israel and Jordan.

19 A committee will be established of representatives of Israel, Jordan, and the Administrative Council to examine existing legislation in Judea, Samaria and the Gaza District, and to determine which legislation will continue in force, which will be abolished, and what will be the competence of the Administrative Council to promulgate regulations. The rulings of the committee will be adopted by unanimous decision.

20 Residents of Israel will be entitled to acquire land and settle in the areas of Judea, Samaria and the Gaza District. Arabs, residents of Judea, Samaria and the Gaza District, who, in accordance with the free option granted them, become Israeli citizens, will be entitled to acquire land and settle in Israel.

21 A committee will be established of representatives of Israel, Jordan, and the Administrative Council to determine norms of immigration to the areas of Judea, Samaria and the Gaza District. The committee will determine the norms whereby Arab refugees residing outside Judea, Samaria and the Gaza District will be permitted to immigrate to these areas in reasonable numbers. The rulings of the committee will be adopted by unanimous decision.

22 Residents of Israel and residents of Judea, Samaria and the Gaza

District will be assured freedom of movement and freedom of economic activity in Israel, Judea, Samaria and the Gaza District.

23 The Administrative Council will appoint one of its members to represent the council before the government of Israel for deliberation on matters of common interest, and one of its members to represent the council before the government of Jordan for deliberation on matters of common interest.

24 Israel stands by its right and its claim of sovereignty to Judea, Samaria and the Gaza District. In the knowledge that other claims exist, it proposes, for the sake of the agreement and the peace, that the question of sovereignty in these areas be left open.

25 With regard to the administration of the holy places of the three religions in Jerusalem, a special proposal will be drawn up and submitted that will include the guarantee of freedom of access to members of all faiths to the shrines holy to them.

26 These principles will be subject to review after a five-year period.

II. EXCERPTS FROM REMARKS BY PRIME MINISTER BEGIN TO THE KNESSET

In paragraph 11 of our plan we stated that security and public order in the areas of Judea, Samaria and the Gaza District will be the responsibility of the Israeli authorities. Without this paragraph the plan for administrative self-rule is meaningless. I wish to state from the Knesset rostrum that this obviously includes the stationing of Israel army forces in Judea, Samaria and the Gaza Strip. It is quite out of the question – if we had been asked to withdraw our army forces from Judea, Samaria and Gaza – to allow these areas to be dominated by the murderers' organization known as the PLO – "Ashaf" in Hebrew translation. This is the vilest organization of murderers in history, with the exception of the Nazi armed organizations. A few days ago it also boasted of the murder of Hamdi el-Qadi, the deputy director of the education office in Ramallah, and today it threatens to solve the problems of the Middle East by one bullet to be dispatched to the heart of Egyptian President Sadat, as its predecessors did in the Al-Aqsa Mosque against King Abdullah – with one bullet. No wonder the

Egyptian government announced that if one such bullet is fired, Egypt will reply with a million bullets.

We want to say that this organization will not be permitted, under any conditions, to dominate Judea, Samaria and Gaza. If we did withdraw our forces, that is what would happen. And therefore let it be known that anyone who wants an agreement with us should be good enough to accept our statement that the Israel Forces will be stationed in Judea, Samaria and Gaza; and there will also be other security arrangements, so that we shall give all the residents – Jews and Arabs in the Land of Israel – the security of life, that is, security for all.

In paragraph 24 we stated: "Israel stands by its right and its claim of sovereignty to Judea, Samaria and the Gaza District. In the knowledge that other claims exist, it proposes, for the sake of the agreement and the peace, that the question of sovereignty in these areas be left open."

We explained this to US President Carter and to Egyptian President Sadat. We have a right and a claim of sovereignty to these areas of the Land of Israel. This is our country, and it belongs by right to the Jewish people. We want agreement and peace. We know that there are at least two other claims of sovereignty over these areas. If there is a mutual will to achieve an agreement and bring about peace, what is the way forward? If these conflicting claims are upheld and if there is no solution to the conflict between them, there can be no agreement between the parties. And for this reason, to facilitate agreement and to make peace, there is only one way: to decide, by agreement, that the question of sovereignty remains open; and to deal with the people, the nations – for the Palestinian Arabs, administrative self-rule; and for the Palestinian Jews, real security. This is the fairness contained in the proposal, and thus it has also been received abroad.

With this plan, as well as with principles which I shall now explain, for settling on relations between Israel and Egypt to be set forth in a peace treaty between these two countries, I went to the United States to visit President Carter and to inform him of both parts of our peace plan. The second part – namely, the principles for the settlement of the relations between Egypt and Israel in the context of a peace treaty – are:

- *Demilitarization* – The Egyptian army shall not cross the Gidi-Mitla line. Between the Suez Canal and this line the agreement for reducing forces shall remain in force.
- *Jewish settlements shall remain in place.* These settlements will be linked with Israel's administration and courts. They will be protected by an Israeli force – and I repeat this sentence for a reason well known to all members of this House – they will be protected by Israeli forces.
- *A transition period of a number of years*, during which IDF forces will be stationed on a defensive line in central Sinai, and airfields, and early-warning installations will be maintained, until the withdrawal of our forces to the international boundary.
- *Guaranteed freedom of navigation in the Straits of Tiran*, which will be recognized by both countries in a special declaration as an international waterway, which must be open to all passage of all ships under any flag; either by a UN force, which cannot be withdrawn except with the agreement of both countries and by unanimous decision of the Security Council, or by joint Egyptian-Israeli patrols.

With the two parts of this peace plan I came to the President of the United States, Mr. Carter. I had a personal *tête-à-tête* with him. Both during that talk and in the talks between the Israeli and American delegations, he expressed a favorable assessment of the plan. On Saturday evening, at the second meeting, the President of the United States said that this plan was a fair basis for peace negotiations. A favorable view of our plan was also expressed by Vice-President Mondale, Secretary of State Vance, the President's adviser on national security and Prof. Brzezinski, as well as the well-known, distinguished and influential Senators Jackson, Case, Javits, Stone, and our dear friend – to whom, on behalf of the entire Knesset of Israel, I today extend best wishes for a full and speedy recovery – Senator Humphrey. In addition, a favorable assessment of this plan was expressed by former US President Gerald Ford, former Secretary of State Henry Kissinger, and the spokesman of the American Jewish community, Rabbi Dr. Schindler. All of them stated that the essence of the plan was its fairness.

From America, *en route* home, I stopped over in London and presented our two-part peace plan to the Prime Minister of Britain and the British Foreign Secretary. Both Mr. Callaghan and Dr. Owen expressed their favorable assessment of our peace plan, and Mr. Callaghan told our Attorney-General that it was a very constructive plan. I also conveyed the plan to the special envoy of the President of the French Republic, Giscard d'Estaing, namely, François Poncet.

While I was in the US, I asked the Secretary of State to contact President Sadat and to inform him, on my behalf, that I would like to meet with him – whether in Cairo or in a neutral place, or, should he so desire, in Ismailiya. I mentioned a meeting in Ismailiya because we spoke of such a possibility with President Sadat when he visited Jerusalem.

The President of Egypt informed me, via the Secretary of State, that he was choosing Ismailiya as the site of our meeting. I agreed. Thus, a few days after the conclusion of my mission in the US and Britain, the meeting in Ismailiya took place.

That was a successful meeting. Its success came with its opening. We held a personal talk, President Sadat and myself, and within the first five minutes of that talk, the decisive result was attained: continuation of the negotiations between the two countries for the signing of a peace treaty – as was decided, instead of the expression "peace agreement" in the meeting between the two delegations in Ismailiya.

These negotiations will be conducted at a high level. The committees will be: political, to sit in Jerusalem, and military, which will sit in Cairo. The chairmen of the committees will be the foreign ministers and the defense ministers of Egypt and Israel. The chairmanship of the committees will rotate. Our foreign minister will begin at the sessions of the committee in Jerusalem. The Egyptian defense minister will begin at the sessions of the military committee in Cairo. At the end of a week, the chairmen will rotate. The political committee will deal with the civilian settlements in the Sinai Peninsula and the subject – which is a moral one, it may be termed an Arab-Jewish one – of the Palestinian Arabs. The military committee will deal with all the military questions connected with the peace treaty for the Sinai Peninsula.

Thus, for the first time in 30 years, in the very near future – about another two weeks – direct, face-to-face negotiations will commence between authorized representatives – ministers of Israel – and Egypt's authorized representatives, its foreign and defense ministers. No third person will serve as chairman of these committees, as was the custom in all the meetings between ourselves and the Arab states; but the ministers themselves will conduct the sessions and rotate as chairmen. These will be fundamental, detailed political and security negotiations for the attainment and signing of peace treaties.

And because this is happening for the first time since the establishment of our state, for the first time after five wars, for the first time after the declarations from various directions that Israel must be liquidated – we must welcome this shift in itself. And let us hope and wish that during the weeks or months that the committees sit they will reach agreement – and if there is an agreement it will serve as a basis for the peace treaty which, in this case, will be signed by authorized representatives of Israel and Egypt.

It may be said that at the Ismailiya meeting the two sides also agreed on a joint declaration. But its publication was prevented because the two delegations did not arrive at an agreed, joint formula for the problem which we term – and justly so – the question of the Palestinian Arabs, while the Egyptians call it, in their terminology – and it is their right to use their terminology – the question of the Palestinian people. We tried, we made an effort, to arrive at a joint formula; but it emerged that we could not accept one or another wording – whether proposed to the Egyptian delegation by us, or whether proposed to the Israeli delegation by the Egyptians. On Sunday, between 10 and 10.30 p.m., we therefore postponed the meeting until Monday morning, on the assumption that, with an effort by both sides, a way out would be found. And, indeed, it was found.

By way of agreement on a joint formula, in accordance with precedents in international conferences, we proposed – and our proposal was accepted – that each side would assert its position and employ its own terminology. Hence, the statement on the question of the Palestinian Arabs, as read out by the President of Egypt to our joint press conference, was made up of two sections, namely: "The position of Egypt is that a Palestinian state should be established in the West Bank and the Gaza Strip. The position of Israel is that the Palestinian Arabs residing in Judea, Samaria and the Gaza District should enjoy self-rule."

Because of the difference over this issue, publication was prevented of the declaration, whose contents had been completely agreed upon. We did not deem it proper to press for publication of a joint statement if the Egyptian side said that under these conditions it could not sign it. But I must note that the content itself was agreed upon by the two delegations together.

MK AHARON YADLIN: How can settlements be defended by an Israeli force if the IDF withdraws to the international border?

PRIME MINISTER BEGIN: That belongs to the debate – and I have learned, especially from committee proceedings – that if someone says he does not understand, he means he does not agree – particularly someone as intelligent as yourself.

Mr. Speaker, with the conclusions from the meeting at Ismailiya, we have done our part; we have given our share. Henceforth, the other side has the floor. For the sake of peace, for the sake of a peace treaty, we have assumed great responsibility and taken many risks. Yes, indeed. And already during these days, since my return from the US, a hard, painful debate has been underway between my best friends and myself. From the Knesset rostrum, too, I shall state, as I told them, that if it is my lot to conduct such a debate, I shall willingly accept the decree. They are my friends. We went a long way together, in difficult days and in good days. I love them, and regard them – and shall continue to regard them – with affection.

But there is no escape. You must accept responsibility with that degree of civic courage without which there can be no political decisions. To me it is clear that we are on the right path to facilitate the negotiations for, and the signing of, a peace treaty. After examining all the other ways, as they have often been mentioned in Knesset debates, I no longer have the slightest doubt that the only way to make negotiations for signing a peace treaty possible is the one that is proposed by the government. Therefore, should it be necessary to face a debate on this matter with dear, even beloved, friends, we shall do so. But it is a fact that the responsibility is great and the risks exist. Therefore I reiterate: in Ismailiya, in the wake of visits to Washington and London, we, the government of Israel, did our part, we made our contribution; and it is now the turn of the other side. If the followers of routine thinking in the Egyptian Foreign Ministry assume that they will succeed in getting international pressure exerted on us, so that we will accept their positions which are unacceptable to us, and that we will agree to them – they are wrong. Even if pressure were to be exerted on us, it would be of no benefit to anyone, because we are used to pressure and the refusal to yield to it.

But I am convinced that no international pressure will be exerted on the State of Israel. It is inconceivable. The persons who praised our peace plan as fair, as constructive, as a breakthrough, are very serious persons. They know its full contents, except for certain amendments – which we have also transmitted to our friends the Americans, and which do not alter the substance of the plan. This is the plan I made known to President Carter and President Sadat. And they cannot, by invitation of the conventional thinkers of the Egyptian Foreign Ministry, change their minds within the space of a few weeks. We have today massive moral support throughout the US: in the administration; in both Houses of Congress – and the House majority leader, Mr. Wright, told me that he praises and approves this peace plan; in American public opinion; and last, but not least, among the American Jewish community.

Therefore the conventional thinkers in the Egyptian Foreign Ministry are making a great mistake if they are under the illusion that if we do not accept their antiquated formulae, which are totally divorced from reality, then international pressure will be exerted on us. It will not. And we shall continue on our path, to bring peace to the people of Israel, to establish peace in the Middle East. For that is my aspiration – not since May and June 1977, but ever since November and December 1947, from the days when – after a break in the relations of peace between the Palestinian Arabs and the Palestinian Jews, the first bullet, directed by an Arab hand into a Jewish heart, was fired, and from the days when I appealed to the Palestinian Arabs from the underground, and called upon them: do not shed Jewish blood, let us build the country together, so that it may be a glorious land for the two peoples. But the bloodshed continued and there were five bloody wars to which we want to put an end by establishing peace and signing peace treaties. This is our heart's desire. And I am certain that I can express the view of the entire house – with the exception, perhaps, of one faction – if I say: this is the heart's desire of the entire Jewish people – to bring peace to the land, having liberated the land.

III. POINTS OF REPLY BY PRIME MINISTER BEGIN TO THE KNESSET DEBATE

When Secretary of State Vance was in Israel I said to him, "What about a meeting with President Sadat?" and he said: "He would like to meet you, too." When I visited Rumania in August, and had talks with Ceaucescu, I raised the possibility of a meeting with the Egyptian president, and he said that at the present stage he would prefer a meeting between representatives, but a personal meeting was also possible. When President Sadat went to Rumania... President Ceaucescu recommended the meeting to him... we were not surprised, there was no shock.

Geula Cohen should ask herself: Perhaps she is wrong? Perhaps this is a good plan, not a bad one? Perhaps it is a Zionist plan and not a danger to the Zionist enterprise? Perhaps this is a plan for a powerful momentum of settlement, and not the stoppage of settlement?

For the first time there is an Israeli peace plan. The whole world is arguing about the Israeli plan, for and against...I am well aware of the power of the Soviet Union...and yet I say: the support of the United States is more important than the opposition of the Soviet Union...we used to be isolated in America and Europe, and now we isolate someone else. This is a most important development...

And now I will tell you about two moments in the Ismailiya conference, in which I was prepared to say to the Egyptian President "*Non possimus*" and to tell my colleagues to be ready to go back home...[A]t

a certain moment we were asked to accept a proposal that Israel under-
takes to withdraw from Judea, Samaria, Sinai, the Golan Heights, and
the Gaza Strip in accordance with the preamble to Resolution 242
emphasizing "the inadmissibility of the acquisition of territory by war."
The debate was dramatic…I told President Sadat that today we are
in Sinai perfectly legitimately…242 does not commit Israel to such a
withdrawal, and therefore we shall not sign such a declaration…and
we were ready to say: if so, we cannot continue. It was agreed that this
paragraph should be eliminated from the joint statement, and we were
able to carry on and prepare a joint statement.

A second moment was when we were called upon…to state that
we agreed to establish a so-called Palestinian state in Judea, Samaria
and Gaza. And again we said: on no account will we accept this. This
would be a deadly danger to the State of Israel…It would also be a
danger to Jordan – "And also a danger to you, Mr. President" – and a
danger to the free world, because of the experience of airlifts to Angola
and Mozambique and Ethiopia, for the flight-time from Odessa to
Bethlehem is less than two hours.

And now I want to explain why we proposed a free choice of
citizenship, including Israeli citizenship…[A]gain the answer is: fairness… we never wanted to be like Rhodesia. And this is a way to show
our fairness to all men of goodwill…here we propose total equality of
rights – anti-racism… – of course, if they chose such citizenship…we
do not force our citizenship on anyone.

Someone tried to be clever and said: This is just a further interim
settlement. There is no basis for this…[I]n general, reconsideration is
possible even before five years have passed. Everyone can make proposals, the Jordanian government can propose, the government of Israel
can do it, the administrative council can do it: let us consider, perhaps
we can add something, or take away something. Actually, this framework of five years is quite incidental…but the agreement is something
new – responsible administration of affairs by the residents in Judea
and Samaria and Gaza through their elected representatives. This is the
meaning of self-rule, and that is why the idea captured the imagination
of people in the free world…

And now I shall discuss the concept of "territorial compromise" with which a part of this house has simply fallen in love: since I fell in love with my wife, I have never seen such love...what is territorial compromise? One part to them and a part to me...it transpires that territorial compromise is the obstacle to peace. If we came to Sadat and told him you will have to sign, and inform the entire Arab world that you agree...to the Jordan rift being under Israeli sovereignty, he would say, on his part, "*Non possimus.*" Thus our idea facilitates agreement and peace, leaving the question of sovereignty open...and so an agreement can be arrived at...[T]he dogmatic, routine, fossilized talk of territorial compromise frustrates every prospect and possibility of conducting negotiations...

QUESTION FROM THE FLOOR: Will there be a plebiscite when the time comes to decide?

PRIME MINISTER BEGIN: There is nothing in our laws about a plebiscite...if there is a majority for a plebiscite I shall of course accept the Knesset's legislation. I have heard that some people propose new elections: I am ready...

Mr. Speaker, the debate has ended. I ask for a vote, and I ask that each and every member of the Knesset, without distinction of faction, vote according to his conscience. There is no imposition, no coercion. I am confident of the result.

IV. THE VOTE BY THE KNESSET

The Knesset vote on the autonomy plan put forward by Prime Minister Begin resulted in 64 voting in favor and 8 against, with 40 abstentions.

One Palestinian People and One Palestine*

Raphael Israeli, *Truman Institute, The Hebrew University of Jerusalem, Jerusalem, Israel*

ABSTRACT: The ten options offered so far to resolve the Palestinian conundrum have proved vain. New thinking that combines Palestinian self-determination rights with Israel's security needs is necessary. The proposed solution rests on the following: (1) mutual acceptance of self-determination for the Palestinians and the Jewish people, (2) mutual recognition of PLO and Zionism, (3) partition of Greater Palestine between Israelis and Palestinians, and (4) separation between sovereignty over territory and personal status of inhabitants.

M ANY SOLUTIONS have been floated around during the past 20 years regarding the problems of the Palestinian people and of the territories in Palestine where they constitute a majority. For this purpose, conventional wisdom has differentiated between the Palestinians living in Israel Proper, the so-called "Israeli-Arabs," as if this were not a contradiction in terms, and the rest of the Palestinians who either have another nationality (Jordanian, Lebanese, and so forth) or are stateless altogether. The former, who used to be considered members of an ethnic-religious-linguistic-cultural minority, have meanwhile turned into a vocal national minority, which, by demanding "equal rights," is claiming joint ownership of Israel by its two constituent peoples and is

---

* This chapter was written in 1985.

actually striving to turn Israel into a bi-national state. The latter have been clamoring for self-determination, for an end to Israeli occupation, and for their own statehood under the leadership of the PLO, which purports to be the sole legitimate representative of all the Palestinians – namely, those under occupation, but also those who maintain Jordanian, Israeli, and other citizenships.

The question of territory has also been confused by the very fact that the territories presently under Israeli administration have been disconnected in Israeli and world public opinion from the eastern part of Palestine, now called Jordan. Thus, on the one hand, Israel has been insistent on treating the "Israeli Arabs" as full-fledged citizens in a Jewish-Zionist state with which they cannot identify, and, on the other hand, it has been disregarding the natural and historical link of all the Palestinians, including those dwelling in Israel, to the land of Greater Palestine. No wonder, then, that all the solutions attempted so far, which detached the Palestinians of the West Bank of the Jordan River (including Israel) from those of the East Bank, fell short of coming to fruition. For with one-third of the Palestinian people in Jordan and one-sixth in Israel, how could anyone produce a comprehensive solution to the Palestinian problem in the West Bank and Gaza alone?

Approximately 10 models of solutions have been created since the 1967 war, and the failure of all of them to gain currency shows how dismal they were in coming to terms with the Palestinian problem in "all its aspects," as promised by the Camp David Accords. If we do not revert to the basic premises of historical Palestine as one unified arena, and of the Palestinian people in all its dispersions as one national unit, neither the Palestinian problem nor the "territories" issue can be laid to rest. That is, there will not be peace and tranquility in the Middle East, now and in the generations to come, unless the conventional wisdom and the accepted norms and notions are challenged, and a less static and more imaginative approach is found.

PERILS OF THE STATUS QUO
Upon the establishment of the State of Israel, a small minority of Palestinian Arabs was "trapped" in what became Israel's sovereign territory

and has since had to reconcile with its new status as a minority. Those Arabs, who were cut off from the rest of the Palestinians for 19 years (1948–1967), were supposed to be loyal to Israel, in return for which they would benefit from all the rights and services that the state affords all its citizens. But neither half of the equation was fulfilled. Moreover, in 1967, when the boundaries of Israel faded away, and more Palestinians came under Israeli rule, the combined bloc of Palestinians, now numbering over two million, posed a new challenge for Israel.

Israel's failure to integrate its Arab citizens became apparent at that time. For, instead of providing them with incentives to become part of the mainstream, by joining the state educational system in Hebrew, by recruiting them into Israel's armed forces, and making them partners to Israel's fate, everything was done to reinforce their separate Arab education in Arabic. They were never asked to pledge allegiance to Israel's flag, and they were excluded from serving in its army, which is the most exciting and integrating experience for all Israeli youth. The consequence is obvious – two separate, not to say antagonistic, societies grew in Israel: one Israeli-Jewish, the other Palestinian-Arab, which is only technically "Israeli." The failure to educate the minority to conform with the ideals and the objectives of the majority has created a distinct sub-society, or anti-society, which cultivated its own desires, norms, and aspirations, feeding upon large and deep strata of frustration and bitterness emanating from unequal opportunities in education, services, economic and political positions of power, and employment in military and security-related industries.

The 1967 war, which eliminated in one stroke the borders between "Israeli Arabs" and their brethren across the "Green Line," has further compounded this already difficult situation and driven it to the point of no return. For although the Arabs in Israel could derive encouragement and pride from their vastly superior economic, educational, and political development, compared with their relatives who were under Jordanian rule until 1967, they were equally boosted by the revelation that they actually were not a minority in the Jewish State, but rather part of an Arab majority that surrounded Israel, and an integral component of the Palestinian people that aspired to its own national independence and territorial integrity. Paradoxically, it was precisely their relatively improved economic and educational position, and the democratic norms that they had internalized within Israeli society, which impelled them to ask for more, and to feel self-confident enough to identify with their Palestinian kin. Thus, they turned from a diffident and self-effacing minority into a vocal and assertive national group. When they demand equal rights, they do it as Israelis who were educated and permitted to clamor for equality, but when it comes to duties involving identification with the Jewish-Zionist state, whose aspirations they cannot share, they invoke their Arab-Palestinian, and sometimes Muslim, identity.

Figures have also resounded loudly in this escalation, for the small and marginal minority of 100,000 in 1949 has now grown to encompass three-quarters of a million people (in 1988, approximately 18% of the total population of Israel), and demographic projections predict that within 15 years, it will attain a figure of one million a quarter (approximately 23% of the population). This large bloc, which constitutes local majorities in the Triangle and the western Galilee, has now voiced the seemingly reasonable claim that the "state belongs to all its inhabitants", which means that Israel is no longer a state of the Jews or a Jewish state, but in fact a Jewish-Arab entity, by virtue of the two national groups living within its confines and holding its passports. The nightmare of a bi-national state begins to lurk on the horizon, even before we add to the equation the Arabs of the territories. Indeed, Land Day, which has been observed by Israeli Arabs since 1976, the emergence of the "Committee of Arab Mayors" that purports to represent all Arabs of Israel, the support that the latter lend to the intifada, and their sporadic acts of sabotage and subversion that are occasionally made public by the Israeli authorities (more than 300 in 1988), ought to ring resounding alarms throughout Israel.

The result is that the "Israeli Arabs" are first of all Arabs and Palestinians, and they identify themselves as such. Israelis who believe that those Arabs are loyal to their country simply take loyalty to mean nonparticipation in acts of sabotage. But this is not the case, for loyal Arabs (and there are certainly and fortunately some of those, too) are not only those who enjoy Israel's democracy and its educational, economic, and health services, but those who are also eager to celebrate its Independence Day, to educate their children in its language and culture, to identify with its Jewish-Zionist goals, and to fight for its security. An Arab who studies at Hebrew University, and operates within the perimeters of law and order, cannot be considered loyal unless he is also prepared to stand night-watch at the student dormitories, just as his Jewish friend would. Arabs in Israel could be considered loyal only if their justified demands for rights and equality of opportunities were coupled with equally fervent demands for equality in national duties.

Yet, another phenomenon makes the status quo untenable, and that is the revival of Islam among the Israeli Arabs, as part of the rising tide of Islamic fundamentalism, some of whose manifestations we see in Iran, Lebanon, the West Bank and Gaza, or even the Rushdie affair and its ramifications. In the recent elections to the local councils in Israel (February 1989), the Islamic Movement in the Arab villages in Israel made impressive gains and became an institutionalized political power that can no longer be ignored (six Arab Councils are headed by Muslim fundamentalists and many other Council members were elected in other towns and villages). Admittedly, the leaders of this movement, who had been arrested in 1980–1981 because of their active participation in sabotage and subversive activities, have learned their lesson and are now operating only within the limitations of law, playing brinkmanship with the farthest boundaries of legality. But there is no doubt that the Islamic state of mind, which is spreading among the Muslims in Israel under the guise of innocent and constructive socio-religious activities, bears a potential irredentist claim vis-à-vis Israel. They have been preparing the ground for that eventuality by setting up "anti-state" institutions of welfare, health, education, and the like.

All these alarming characteristics of the Arabs in Israel pale in comparison with the much more frightening issue of the more numerous and less submissive Palestinians in the territories. Their numbers (over 1.5 million in 1988)[1], their formal foreign affiliation (all of them hold non-Israeli passports), and their national consciousness, which is at a

---

1 In 2002, over 3.5 million

much higher pitch, are all expressed in the intifada. They have well taken advantage of the presence of Israel, under whose occupation they have enjoyed newly established universities, a dramatic rise in technological development and in living standards, new norms of democracy and freedom, the breakdown of archaic social structures, and the adoption of new sociopolitical forms of organization. At the same time, however, they wished to preserve and cultivate their own identity, they developed their own local and national leadership which, as a whole, identified with the PLO, and never lost sight of their occupied status, and its corollaries of resistance and struggle. Those Arabs, who have continued to educate their children according to Jordanian curricula and to resort to the Jordanian-style administrative and judicial systems, are, as could be expected, even less loyal to Israel than the "Israeli Arabs." Moreover, the intifada, which burst out in December 1987, has become enough of a continuous, sustained, and wide-scale movement to spell out their irresistible ambition to become independent and to rid themselves of what they regard as Israeli occupation. These aspirations are, naturally, fed by the sweeping tide of Palestinian nationalism, and to no less an extent by the overbearing enthusiasm of the fundamentalist Hamas movement, which regards as its ultimate goal the establishment of an Islamic state over the entire area of Palestine.

The Israeli Arabs who do not belong to the Islamic Movement are likely to demand secession from Israel in the long run, based on the right of self-determination of the Palestinian people of which they are a part. This claim would be reinforced if Israel maintained its rule over the territories, for then the combined population of Arabs under Israeli rule would amount to 40% – that is, Israel would become a de facto bi-national state. The proponents of the Islamic movement on both sides of the "Green Line" have already begun preparing for their Islamic state and have set up the necessary machineries to take over when they are afforded the opportunity. In the West Bank and Gaza, Hamas has unabashedly launched a challenge to the PLO and has stated its plan to establish no less than a full-fledged Islamic state under its aegis. All this means that anyone who advocates the maintenance of the status quo is dreaming. All those who believed that the Arabs of Israel and of the territories could be held, indefinitely, under Israeli control, have been proved wrong. The situation is worsening almost daily, although there is an occasional respite. At times, it is possible to reduce the level of violence or to reduce the riots in the West Bank from a menace to a nuisance level, but the general trend seems inexorable. Therefore, there is no merit to seeking interim solutions that could only postpone the day of reckoning. One needs to devise a fundamental solution that would encompass all, or most, Palestinian Arabs, and finally bring about peace and tranquility to all.

PALESTINIZATION OF JORDAN

The not unfounded allegation was advanced that the territory east of the Jordan River, now called Jordan, is part of historical Palestine. The fact that the British mandatory power decided to sever that territory, which constitutes three-quarters of Palestine, and to give it another name, does not diminish one iota of its historical and geographical belonging to Palestine. Moreover, viewed in present-day practical terms, and not only in historical terms, the so-called Jordanians are actually Palestinians, not only because they are of Palestine but principally because two-thirds of them identify themselves as Palestinians. True, the UN Partition Resolution of 1947, which lent international legitimacy to the State of Israel, applied to the territory west of the river, but if we tackle the problem today on the fashionable basis of "self-determination," there is no denying that the people of Jordan are Palestinians, in their majority at the very least. Prime ministers, such as Zaid Rifai, are Palestinians, many cabinet ministers are Palestinians, and most of the population of Amman, the capital, defines itself as Palestinian. Because the PLO purports to represent all Palestinians, and most Palestinians accept it as their sole representative, it can easily claim, on the basis of "self-determination," that Jordan is, actually, Palestine. All that needs to be done, according to this view, is to dub Jordan "Palestine," and the problem would, thereby, be resolved.

But the issue is more complicated than that, because Jordan is home to only one third of the Palestinian people (more than 1.8 million out of five million)[2], while most of them reside under Israeli rule (1.5 million in the territories and three-quarters of a million in Israel proper in 1988). As long as this large mass of Palestinians identifies itself as such and recognizes the PLO as its leader, it will remain the center of gravity of Palestinian national life without which no Palestinian state can be established or survive. "Israeli Arabs" often claim that the PLO does not represent them, and that they regard themselves as the inhabitants of Israel even if there should be a Palestinian state. But, at the same time, they also claim that the PLO is the "sole representative of the Palestinians"; if they recognize the PLO and its platform, they, by necessity, also accept it as their representative.

Those who support Palestinization of Jordan hope that if the PLO should take over in Amman, as they were close to doing during "Black September" in 1970, then the allegation that it is Israel that prevents self-determination from the Palestinian people would be dispelled. But this is not the case, for even in such an eventuality, Israel would continue to rule most of the "unliberated" Palestinians, and, far from laying the problem to rest, the Palestinian case would gain more impetus, using the Jordanian territory as a precedent, in order to demand self-determination not only in the West Bank and Gaza, but also in the Triangle and the Galilee in Israel proper. Thus, this solution holds no promise for Israel.

JORDANIZATION OF PALESTINE

Others support the mirror-image of the first solution – namely returning to the status quo ante bellum of 1967 by returning the West Bank, or most of it, to Jordan. Some Israeli politicians have raised the notion of functional partition between Israel and Jordan, with the former maintaining security control and the latter taking charge of the domestic affairs of the Palestinians to rid them of Israeli occupation and to satisfy their yearning to be ruled by Arabs. At the basis of this concept is the assumption that King Hussein is moderate, pro-Western, and that he

---

2 In 2002, over 3.5 million

would control the Palestinians better and more effectively than Israel, without, however, posing a threat to Israel.

A variation of this thinking spoke about a territorial compromise, as part of the Jordanian option. The Allon Plan, for example, is considered a manifestation par excellence of this approach – that is, to return to Jordan the non-vital and thickly populated areas of the West Bank, while Israel retains the strategic grounds that are also thinly populated by Palestinians. Everyone knows, however, that such an option never existed in the world of reality, except for three weeks between June 8, 1967, when Israel took over East Jerusalem, and June 28, when Israel annexed it. For since that date, and during all the dialogues, meetings, and exchanges of messages between Israeli leaders and King Hussein, the Jordanians have adamantly refused any peace settlement that would not encompass all "occupied territories, including East Jerusalem." Where was that "Jordanian option" then, except in the world of illusion of some Israeli statesmen?

Even had King Hussein accepted the Israeli view of territorial compromise, that would not have resolved the thorny issue of self-determination, which is paramount in the eyes of Palestinians and without which no permanent solution can be envisaged. At most, this approach could have resolved Hussein's problems, but that should not be Israel's concern, because that "moderate" and "pro-Western" ruler, none other, did not hesitate to use American tanks and guns to attack western Jerusalem in June 1967, despite Israel's supplications that he should keep out of the war. But he thought that he could ride the Egyptian bandwagon to victory and thus triggered the disaster that befell him. After that war, when the Americans refused to supply him with Hawk missiles, he did not hesitate to turn to the Soviet Union and to acquire batteries of their SAM's.

For years the government of Israel, like the rest of the world, except for Britain and Pakistan, had insisted that Hussein's rule in the West Bank was illegal. How could Israel, then, negotiate the fate of those territories with someone who had never gained legitimacy for his annexation of those lands? Moreover, Hussein himself has accepted the notion of the PLO as the sole representative of the Palestinians, and he has undertaken to submit to Palestinian rule any "liberated" part of their territory. In June 1988, when Hussein finally recognized the inconsistency of his own policy and announced the severance of Jordan from the West Bank, he thereby confirmed that any territories he would receive from Israel would be turned over to the Palestinians. Thus, the "Jordanian option" has become a "PLO option". Is this what Israel wanted to achieve? Hussein himself has been facing serious problems of legitimacy for his autocratic rule in Jordan over a Palestinian majority. Why should Israel lend a hand to that outdated and undemocratic government that is tottering on the brink of collapse under the weight of its own inconsistencies and illegitimacy? Why should Israel conclude a deal with a proprietor who has long ago forfeited his right and possession over the asset Israel wants to negotiate away?

THE PLO STATE

The Palestinian state, which was declared on November 15, 1988, in Algiers, might appear to be a satisfactory attempt to resolve the Palestinian problem. However, judging by their insistence on the right of return, their continued commitment to "armed struggle", their persistent negation of Zionism, and their inability or unwillingness to abrogate the offensive and subversive items (to Israel) of the Palestinian Charter, it is clear that the PLO has not reconciled yet to the idea of an independent Jewish State of the Jewish people, by the Jewish people, and for the Jewish people. Therefore, a PLO-dominated state in the West Bank and Gaza would be a recipe for instability, irridentism, and subversion against Israel. Moreover, with Arab rejection-front backing, the PLO is bound to seek to gain control over all of West Palestine and then East Palestine, to "liberate" all components of the scattered Palestinian people, and to set up a greater Palestinian state that would encompass most Palestinians. Palestinian ambition to use the incremental policy of stages, adopted in 1974, and spelling out the plan to use any "liberated" part of Palestine as a launching pad to liberate the rest, has never been abrogated or amended, neither explicitly nor implicitly. But this is not the point, for even if the PLO meant every word and pledge it undertook, and even if it should content itself with a mini-Palestinian state, its very claim to represent all Palestinians, while its state encompasses only one-third of them, would signify that two-thirds of the problem would remain unresolved. This would, in turn, imply that acts of terror, bitterness against truncated Palestine, and dreams of eliminating Israel in the long run would militate against such a settlement. It is necessary to reject the PLO claim that asserts that the mini-state would only constitute a refuge to some of the Palestinians while the others, like the Jewish Diaspora, would continue to live outside it. This comparison has no leg to stand on, because most Jews in the Diaspora live in open, democratic, and prosperous countries and do not wish, for the moment, to move to Israel, which is eager to accept them in its midst. Most Palestinians, on the contrary, live in refugee camps or under autocratic regimes in the Middle East, and they would continue to knock on the doors of a Palestinian state, which would be unable to absorb them. Palestinians would be all the more impelled to seek Palestinian citizenship because many of them are stateless in Arab countries, except for Jordan (which is part of Palestine in any case). Thus, a mini-state would constitute a mini-solution and no more.

There are other crucial considerations militating against a shrunken Palestinian state in the West Bank and Gaza, such as the unrealistic Palestinian demand that Israeli settlements be dismantled and removed. For, in principle, exactly as there are many Arab settlements within Israel proper, there is no reason that Jewish settlements cannot exist within the densely populated Arab areas of Palestine. Another problem is demilitarization which, for many Israelis, is as a matter of course. There is no assurance, however, that the Palestinians could reconcile to remaining powerless and without a military force as one of the major paraphernalia of independence, in view of the prominence of armed forces everywhere. (See, for example, postwar Japan, which already maintains a strong "self-defense force" despite its commitment to renounce, "forever", military power.) And what if any independent Palestinian state should invite foreign troops to its soil, Arab or otherwise? Could Israel resist or go to war? And what if such troops are marched into the Palestinian state

under the auspices of a major power? Would anyone come to Israel's
succor or condone an Israeli act of war to scuttle such a danger?

AUTONOMY AND FEDERATION

In 1972, King Hussein proposed the idea of autonomy for the Palestinians in the West Bank, within his reputed "Federation Plan". The king's
intent then was to regain control of the territories he lost in 1967 by
paying lip service to some sort of Palestinian "independence". In fact,
that plan was geared to make the Palestinians masters of their domestic
affairs, while the source of authority and sovereignty would lie with the
Hashemite Crown, so that Jordanians would legitimize Palestinians, not
the other way around, despite the overwhelming majority of Palestinians (over 80%) in such a federated state. Foreign and security matters
would remain the domain of the central government in Amman. This
solution, if implemented, could have had enormous advantages, for it
would have ensured a stable government in the long run and would have
guaranteed the participation of Palestinians in the federal government.
No wonder, then, that the Reagan Plan of September 2, 1982, and then
the Shultz Initiative of 1988, devised variations of that theme.

The Israeli government suggested the mirror-image of the Federation Plan, that is autonomy, as an interim settlement, but deriving its
authority from the Israeli legislature. But the Autonomy Plan of Camp
David, which followed this pattern of thought, did not offer quite the
same advantages as the Federation Plan. On the one hand, it was to be
a temporary agreement, not a permanent one; and it did not provide
the Palestinians with any place in the determination of Greater Israel's
affairs. It did determine that Israel would retain control of foreign and
security affairs while the Palestinians would manage their own domestic
domain. On the other hand, the Israeli Plan was more generous, inasmuch as it left open the possibility of a Palestinian state following the
interim period of autonomy, which would last from three to five years,
while the Jordanian Federation Plan was to exclude terminally the
question of Palestinian independence. The appeal of this Israeli plan is
what resuscitated it in the form of mayoral elections in the West Bank
and Gaza, as spelled out by the Israel government in 1989.

But both of these alternatives for autonomy were rejected by the Palestinians, because neither of them responds to their basic aspiration for self-determination and for an independent Palestinian state. These substitutes seemed, perhaps, a good solution to Jordan's or to Israel's problems, but not to the Palestinian plight. The Palestinians still remember the trauma of September 1970, when King Hussein massacred thousands of them, and they are not likely to throw in their lot with him. This is all the more so since the king himself has accepted the 1974 Rabat decision to recognize the PLO as the sole representative of the Palestinians and has detached himself from the heartland of Palestine in 1988, as a result of the intifada. The Israeli Autonomy Plan was agreed upon only by Israel, Egypt, and the United States, but the last two partners have disassociated themselves from it in the meantime. Europeans and the rest of the Arabs have never accepted this plan of Israel's because they did not believe that it was either feasible or desirable.

And, most important, the "Declaration of Independence" of the Palestinians on November 15, 1988, has foreclosed the road before the Palestinians to accept anything short of their independence. Any attempt by Israel to enforce one-sided autonomy, as Moshe Dayan had suggested, would not bring about peace and tranquility, exactly as a forced marriage cannot produce conjugal harmony. Therefore, if marriage by love is impossible, one could at the very least aspire to a marriage of expediency, based on the mutual interests of both parties. No peace is possible between Israel and the local leadership of the Palestinians in the territories because of the inherent contradiction between the nationalists and ultra-religious factions on the one hand, and those who are likely to embrace the Autonomy Plan, while the majority rejects it, on the other.

ANNEXATION AND TRANSFER OF POPULATION

The above options have discussed "Jordanization" and "Palestinization," but there is also an "Israelization" one. Contrary to the maximalist and intransigent image that was attached to this alternative, which would involve outright annexation of the territories by Israel, one could defend it as precisely responding to the Israeli Left's slogan of "territory for peace". But the departure point of the proponents of this plan is totally different: they are prepared to renounce three-quarters of the land of historical Palestine east of the Jordan in return for peace, but they seek to retain that one-quarter of the land west of the river, without which, in their mind, Israel could not ensure its national and security existence.

But this approach has not been adopted by the majority of Israelis despite its being seemingly conciliatory. The reason is demographic: most Israelis would retain the territories if they were not populated by the 1.5 million[3] Palestinians who reject Israel's rule. But even if they had accepted Israel's government (as Dr. Nusseibeh has suggested in recent years, provided the one-man one-vote principle is maintained), the Israelis would be faced with an intractable dilemma: either a democratic and egalitarian Israel with rights for all, with the corollaries of a bi-national state immediately and an Arab majority state in the future; or a Jewish Israel where the Jews would maintain rights and rule and the Arabs would be devoid of both. No Israeli government could face that dilemma and resolve it in any acceptable way.

In this regard, one may observe one of the most fascinating paradoxes in the Israeli political culture: the Israeli Liberal Left and the Civil Rights watchers are precisely those who fear that they could not envisage a bi-national state and, therefore, press for disengaging from the territories and maintaining the Jewish nature of the State; conversely, the adamant right wing nationalists view with disdain the pessimistic outlook of the Left and can envisage a Greater Israel where Jews and Arabs can coexist in full equality. In this momentous debate there are unstated arguments as well: those who want to relinquish the territories view the question of Jewish majority as so overbearing that they elect to be dubbed "defeatists" by some, "racists" by others, rather than face the prospects of oppressing civil rights in a country where Arabs might jeopardize the Jewish majority. The Right is prepared to swallow the accusation that it accepts diluting the Jewish majority and ruling another people, rather than to imply that it would give up any

---

3 In 2002, over 3 million

part of Eretz Israel or have to restrict Arab civil rights when the Jewish majority is threatened.

Thus, regardless of whether or not the arguments are stated, the overwhelming consideration bearing on annexation is demography. No one can control or even predict the rate of population growth of the Palestinian Arabs, especially as the Palestinians, both in Israel and in the territories, have become aware of the "demographic war" and are pinning their hopes on it for deciding the future of Palestine. Therefore, the idea of "transfer" was evoked by some ultra-rightist Israelis as the only solution to Israel's dilemma and to the Palestinian demographic menace. Transfer of Palestinian populations to neighboring Arab countries, they reason, is necessary to maintain Israel's rule on the territories without endangering either the Jewish or the democratic character of the country.

Much of the outrage of the Israeli public against such a solution emanates from moral sensitivity to the horrifying prospect of uprooting a civilian population from its land and moving it elsewhere. But people remain oblivious to the idea of transfer that is inherent in the Palestinian National Charter, which envisages that only the Jews who were in Palestine before 1917 ("the beginning of the Zionist onslaught") would be allowed to remain. This means that the rest – that is everyone except for those 80,000 pioneering Zionists, most of whom are dead by now in any case, would have, if not somehow to evaporate, to be transferred back to their countries of origin, if they should survive the "armed struggle" that the Charter pledges in order to regain Palestine. Compared with this sinister prospect, the Israeli transfer plan would be much milder if carried out, and at the very least would constitute an ideological counteract to ambitions, if it is not. To this argument one could add, of course, that thousands of Jews were already transferred from the Arab countries into Israel in the 1950s and the 1960s. Since the Palestinians are claiming that they are part of the Arab homeland, one could interpret the two transfers as an exchange of population, not as a one-sided forced transfer by Israel.

Joseph Schechtman, the greatest authority on population transfers, who researched the exchanges of populations in Europe after World

War One, has set standards for the morality of this otherwise abhorrent measure. All the criteria he determined as justifying a transfer are handily applicable to the Israeli-Arab situation, and they can be summarized in the following rule: if there are no prospects for reconciliation and harmony between the ruling majority and the ruled minority, and if there is no practical way to separate territorially the minority from the majority, it is far more moral to uproot the minority and transfer it elsewhere, despite the terrible suffering and injustice caused to this generation in the process, than to cause suffering and injustice to both the majority and the minority in all generations to come.

The problem is not moral, but political and practical. In order to transfer a large population from one country to another with a minimum of suffering, one needs two prerequisites: that the population in question agrees to move and that a host country be prepared to absorb them (for example, Turks of Bulgaria these days). Those two conditions were met when 800,000 Jews, including the present writer, were transferred from the Arab countries to Israel. But with Palestinians the situation is different: they have been cultivating the value of *Sumud* (steadfastness) in their clinging to the soil, and there is no Arab state ready or willing to absorb them. Therefore, short of war or of a bloodbath of untold proportions, transfer as a solution is simply a pipedream with no relation to reality.

SQUARING THE TRIANGLE

It is evident, then, that a novel option is needed to weave some of the positive elements of the other options into a strong fabric that would respond to the most vital interest of the three entities where Palestinians dwell today: Israel, Jordan, and the territories. A novel solution is needed not because of the intifada or because of outside pressures on Israel, but simply because all other options, some of which have been negotiated for years, have failed to produce even the beginning of a permanent settlement. From Israel's point of view, instead of facing world opinion defensively, in an attempt to thwart the image of rejection that is associated with its policy, it could turn things around by seizing the initiative and proclaiming a daring and generous new plan that would not diminish Israel's security. Its principal components could be:

THE PALESTINIAN PEOPLE'S RIGHT TO SELF-DETERMINATION

The Palestinians, the absolute majority of whom is in Jordan (over 1.5 million), in the territories (1.5 million)[4], and in Israel (three-quarters of a million)[5], with the rest in refugee camps or in close and distant diasporas, are entitled to Israel's recognition and aid to realize their basic aspirations. In return, they ought to recognize a parallel right of the Jewish people to self-determination in their Jewish state. This is a crucial element that Israel ought to insist on, because this is precisely what the Palestinian National Charter denies. That Palestinian constitutional document, which was never abrogated, in fact states that Judaism is a faith, and, therefore, Jews are not a nation, implying that they do not deserve a state. Recognizing the State of Israel's right to exist, in this context, would not be sufficient because, according to the PLO logic, which is supported by the majority of Palestinians everywhere, the State of Israel, which belongs to all of its inhabitants, would become another Palestinian state in the long run after Israel retreats to the 1947 Partition boundaries, and the Right of Return of the Palestinians would be implemented.

There is, of course, a different problem facing Israel, regarding the representatives of the Palestinians with whom it has to negotiate. The Palestinians have arguably chosen the PLO, and it is certainly their right, because they consider it as their movement of national liberation. But Israel can refuse to talk with such an interlocutor as long as it continues to condemn and denigrate the movement of national liberation of the Jewish people – Zionism – as "racist", and continues to discredit and delegitimize it in its unaltered Charter and in the Algiers Declaration. The rhetorical advances uttered toward Israel in recent months do not include even a hint reversing that direction. If anything, the Fatah

---

4 In 2002, over 3.5 million
5 In 2002, over 1 million

Conference held in Tunis in August 1989 even reinforced the old clichés. As long as this is the case, Israel can offer to talk to the 2.5 million Palestinians under its rule (in Israel and the territories), about the peace plan outlined below. If they concur, they would thereby signify a break with the Charter. If they do not, the burden of proof shifts to them.

THE PALESTINIANS' RIGHT OVER PALESTINE

The Palestinians claim a right over all of Palestine, exactly as the Israelis do. Therefore, the only feasible solution is a mutual recognition of that right, from which derives the necessity to partition the land. In other words, Greater Palestine (or Eretz Israel) will have to be divided by agreement between its two proprietors into an Israeli-Jewish state in the West and a Palestinian-Arab state in the East. It does not stand to reason that three quarters of the land be severed from it and called by another name (Jordan), while the remaining quarter should become the object of a new partition. We have seen that this approach is anchored in both history and demography. If the Palestinians today want a state, they ought to demand it from the autocratic king from the Hijaz who has been ruling three-quarters of their land and one-third of their people who constitute the majority of the population there. If they want to be loyal to the king and keep him, it is their affair; if the king wishes to test his long-standing claim that he is beloved of his subjects and is popular with them, they would certainly consent to turn their state into the "Hashemite Kingdom of Palestine" and their king into a constitutional monarch, while the Palestinian majority retains the actual governmental authority.

This is the government, whatever its composition, that Israel would have to deal with on the implementation of this peace plan. The negotiations will then be protracted, difficult, and tortuous regarding the final boundaries between them. This argument, however, would be a quantitative one about territory and assets that can be agreed upon in the process of give-and-take as a means and compromise as an end. It would no longer be a qualitative conflict between Israel and the rest of the world over whether a Palestinian state should exist. Such a Palestinian state would not, by nature, be any stronger than present-day

Jordan. And if this "moderate" Jordan could attack Israel in 1967, and is now able to bring into its borders Iraqi, Saudi, and Syrian divisions to battle Israel, there is no reason for Israel to fear that a Palestinian state would be a worse threat. The fate of the territories now held by Israel will then be discussed not with King Hussein, a proposition to which all Israeli governments have committed themselves, but with the Palestinian government based in Amman, which is Israel's true co-owner of the land. In the past, Israel has denied the king's right to claim sovereignty over the territories. What gives him more of a right today after he has detached himself from that claim?

When such a state is established, the PLO will become redundant, even if its present leaders should be elected to lead its government. The Palestinian government would then become, with or without the Hashemite king, Israel's partner for negotiation not only about the territories but also about the permanent status of the Palestinian population, presently under Israel. This government would be recognized by Israel, provided that it drops its ideology of pursuing "armed struggle" (those are the terms of the Charter) and not only "renounces terrorism"; recognizes the right of self-determination of the Jewish people, Zionism as the movement of national liberation of the Jews, and the principle of partition of Greater Palestine. Until such a Palestinian state evolves, Israel can cultivate the idea among the 2.3 million Palestinians under its rule and even assist them in attaining hegemony in Amman, should the king refuse to compromise with them by giving up some of his absolute authority in favor of the majority in his country.

A NOVEL DEFINITION OF SOVEREIGNTY

This necessity would establish a distinction between ownership of territory and the personal status of the inhabitants, to respond to the contradictory desires of the Palestinians for self-determination and statehood for the Palestinians on the one hand, and the acute security needs of Israel, which would make a major withdrawal impractical on the other. In other words, regardless of the contours of the permanent boundaries agreed upon between Israel and Palestine, many Palestinians would remain under Israeli rule all i.e. "Israeli Arabs" of today and probably most inhabitants of the territories. They could choose among three options:

- To sell their property and move east into the Palestinian state, where they can build the future of their choice;
- To acquire Israeli citizenship by a series of symbolic and practical acts that would put their loyalty to the state beyond doubt: oath of allegiance to the flag, identification with the Jewish-Zionist state, educating their children in Hebrew in the state mixed school systems, and military service in its armed forces. In this case, they should be guaranteed all the rights accruing to Israel's Jewish nationals; or
- To stay as alien residents in Israel and enjoy its advantages: freedom, democracy, prosperity, services, as long as they abide by the law and pay their taxes, but they would owe their political loyalty to the neighboring Palestinian state where they could also express their personal political ambitions by voting and running for office. In a situation of peace and open boundaries between Israel and Palestine, the Arabs who would opt for this alternative (presumably the majority, including Israeli Arabs) would move freely to and fro, similar to Canadians in the United States, with minimal checking procedures on the border check-points. They would have realized their ambitions for freedom, independence, and statehood, and they would not have to vacate their present towns and villages. It is likely that in the far future, when the Palestinian state is well established, peaceful, and prosperous, many Palestinian Arabs still under Israeli rule would opt to move there. But even if they do not, the distances are small enough to make practical the cleavage between the country of residence and the country of allegiance. Those who would remain in Israel as foreign aliens, but would opt, at the same time, to pursue acts of terror or of disturbing public order, can be "repatriated" (not "expelled").

In principle, Israel must recognize the reciprocity of this arrangement, under the theoretical assumption that during the negotiations upon the final status of the territory, the present day Israeli settlements there might come under discussion. Under the principle of reciprocity, it can be agreed that the inhabitants of the settlements that might fall within Palestinian sovereignty would enjoy the same choice among the three options offered to the Palestinians. The principle of reciprocity would also allow Israel to increase the pace of settlement building in the West Bank and Gaza, as an added incentive to peace. For in a situation where three-quarters of a million[6] Palestinians live in Israel proper, prior to the permanent settlement, and many more would stay under Israel subsequent to the settlement, the present-day 80,000[7] Israeli settlers in the territories claimed by the Palestinians are only a small fraction compared to the Palestinians in Israel. Thus, the closer Israel comes to parity with Palestine in the pattern of settlement within the population of the other side, the higher the stakes and the more pressing the interest that both parties would have to maintain peace after the settlement is signed. Perhaps, then, Israel would have also to revise its Law of Return to signify that Israeli citizenship is acquired, universally, by those who perform symbolic acts of identification and practical acts of service to the state, and not automatically granted to any Jew who arrives in Israel.

BALANCE OF GAINS AND DRAWBACKS

This sort of solution cannot satisfy all desires of all parties. Each party would be distressed by the disadvantages inherent in such a settlement, but it could also cheer at the prospects that it promises. Each party will find that it pays a price (a heavy one at that) for achieving its aims, but also that most of its vital ambitions would be achieved. Perhaps this is the most promising formula for a permanent peace treaty between Israelis and Palestinians. For peace, like any other commodity, bears a price tag, and it is apparent that the other options proposed in the international exchange of ideas carry price tags that are far too expensive. Let us consider the goods accruing to every party as well as the required price.

Israel, at the price of totally and finally renouncing eastern Palestine,

---

6 In 2002, over 9 million
7 In 2002, 250,000

and even negotiating the fate of the territories it now holds west of the Jordan River, would achieve most of its desires: it would keep most of the strategic areas west of the river to satisfy its security needs, while the demographic menace against the constitution of the state would be neutralized; the Palestinian Arabs under Israeli rule, once they are assured of statehood, nationhood, and freedom of choice in their future, would calm down and desist from violence; the problem of Israeli Arabs, who are torn between their country and their people, would be resolved and each individual would be the master of his or her own fate; Israel could then regain the image of a peace-loving and generous country, once its crucial contribution to Palestinian independence is proven; Israel's eastern border would be secure and peaceful; it would be able to remain a Jewish democratic state, free from the demographic menace; Israel's improved peaceful boundaries would render it an attractive place for other Jews around the world; and Israeli settlements in the territories would not only be maintained, but they could even be reinforced under the reciprocity rule invoked above.

The Palestinians, who also claim the right to all of Palestine, would have to compromise by ceding to Israel most of the territory west of Jordan. They would likewise have to abrogate or alter the Charter, so that the "Right of Return" and "armed struggle" are amended and an accommodation of the Jewish Zionist state is adopted. In return, they would get three quarters of historical Palestine, where plenty of territory is available for resettling refugees who have been languishing in run-down camps for the past 40 years. They would finally have a state of their own and gain Israel's recognition and safe boundaries with her. They would control the fate of most Palestinians, either directly through Palestinian rule over them, or indirectly, via citizenship to those dwelling in Israel and elsewhere. They could enjoy Israeli technical and economic aid, and Israel's collaboration in trade, labor markets, ports to the Mediterranean, and help against common enemies who would not reconcile with the Israeli-Palestinian peace. They would, in short, be able to channel their enormous energies, talent, manpower, and creativity to developing their country, resettling their refugees, and cultivating their heritage and culture. They would also be able to enjoy a large and strong army posted east of the Jordan River, which would pose no threat to Israel.

The Jordanian Royal House would have to renounce a large part of its ruling authority and become a constitutional monarchy, in recognition that "popular will" in today's Jordan is expressed by the Palestinian population that constitutes the majority there. Certainly, no ruler has ever relinquished power of his own volition, but this would be a much smaller sacrifice than the territorial and ideological concessions that both Israel and the Palestinians would be called upon to make. In return, the king would, perhaps, be able to regain some lost parts of his kingdom; he would double, or more, the number of his subjects, enjoy full legitimacy as head of a "Hashemite Palestinian" state whose government represents the preponderance of the Palestinians inside and outside the kingdom. He would enjoy peace with Israel and stability for his crown, and would be able to devote his energies to government, culture, and economic matters as a reigning, but not governing head of state. He could, perhaps, even retain some authority as supreme commander of the armed forces; he could dissolve the parliament, nominate the government, and the like. If he is so sure of his popularity among his subjects, he could even abdicate his throne and run for election as head of state or prime minister.

It is evident that if such a plan were announced by Israel, it would immediately be rejected as a nonstarter by the Palestinians and the king. Therefore, it is vital that the United States and Arab countries such as Saudi Arabia and Egypt, which carry much influence in Jordan and control much of its livelihood, should first adopt the plan or a variation of it as a basis for negotiations, before it is presented to the world. When King Hussein is then faced with the painful choice of either losing everything or compromising with the Palestinians and Israel, he might consider this option. So might the Palestinians, who can only gain from a settlement of this sort, and so might Israel, which can be talked into such a solution. The most vital interests of all parties are served and, therefore, they are likely to make the required concessions. This proposal would then create the necessary ambiance to produce other, similar solutions along the other borders with Israel after the

Palestinian powder keg had been defused and the Palestinian settlement is alive, breathing, and kicking (gently and creatively). Then, all sorts of other regional arrangements could be dreamt of, such as federations, confederations, common markets, and even security pacts. This can be done only after the Palestinians have savored the taste of freedom and independence. Only then would they be sufficiently self-confident to consider sacrificing part of it for the sake of establishing larger supra-state organizations. Only then could the Middle East march toward new horizons that are unimaginable today.

It is possible that the present solution is far from perfect, but the others are even worse. Great statesmanship consists of seizing the imperfect, the difficult, and the uncomfortable before it becomes unfeasible and impossible. Otherwise, we are all bound to embark on an impasse that could only lead to more war and bloodshed. Perhaps the intifada, which has rendered Palestinian suffering even more unbearable, can be the turning point that will prove to everyone that the tragic Palestinian Triangle consisting of Jordan, Israel and the Palestinians can be finally squared.

The Canton Alternative

Raphael Israeli

IMMEDIATELY FOLLOWING THE 1967 War, when the West Bank and Gaza came under Israeli rule, and before the widespread pattern of Israeli settlements made the wholesale return of the territories to some Arab entity impractical, plans and ideas were rife regarding the eventual/desirable disposition of those lands, if and when an agreed settlement would be reached. At the time, especially after the three No's of Khartoum, where the Arab world indicated that it was in no mood to negotiate, let alone agree, with Israel on anything, the prospects seemed remote and detached from any reality that could be envisioned on the political horizon of those days. Among the original free-thinkers then, who included Yigal Allon, the author of the famous Allon Plan, was also Ra'anan Weitz, a man of vision and extraordinary experience in land and rural planning. In his capacity as the Head of the Settlement Department of the Jewish Agency and the Zionist Federation, he was responsible for many major settlement projects throughout Israel.

RA'ANAN WEITZ'S PLAN

Weitz's plan rested on the basis of maintaining the territory of West Palestine as one federal unit, wherein government would be de-centralized and delegated to local authorities who would assume the responsibility for the affairs of the populations under their jusridiction, in the framework of autonomous cantons. According to the plan, the entire land was to be divided into eight cantons, five preponderantly Jewish, along more-or-less the existing administrative lines of division of the State of Israel, and three preponderantly Arab – one in the Gaza Strip and two dividing the West Bank into north and south, the separation being around Jerusalem, which would remain a special-status area.

The plan also envisaged the return to cantonized Israel of a certain number of Palestinian 1967 refugees, to be settled in a new agricultural development project in the Dotan Valley area near Jenin, and another similar development project south of Hebron, to help ease the density of the population in the Gaza Strip. A new industrial zone was to be established in the vicinity of Nablus, to provide for industrialization of, and employment in the future Palestinian canton.

Each canton, according to Weitz's vision, would enjoy autonomy and administer its own internal affairs, in the areas of development and social services – education, health, social welfare, religious affairs and the like – while a federal government, like that of Switzerland, would take control of national security, foreign affairs and finance, and at the same time supervise the functioning of the cantons and coordinate their activities. The division between five overwhelmingly Jewish and three Arab cantons, would ensure a permanent Jewish majority in the federal government. This cantonal organization would ideally also promote the emergence of a responsible local leadership, which would address the problems of its constituency separately from national concerns, as well as provide a pool for the growth of Jewish and Arab national leaders.

The plan allows for direct financial and economic links between the Arab cantons and potential sources of support in the Arab world, as well as with international bodies. The massive compensations to the refugees would create enough investment capital to energize the economy and contribute to its development apace, thus gradually reducing gaps between Jewish and Arab cantons, and speeding up the process of refugee resettlement and rehabilitation. This would also diminish Arab dependence on the Jewish labor market and help shrink the areas of friction between the partners to the federation.

Socially and politically, Arab autonomy in their own cantons should allow for their intelligentsia to find expression in local or federal politics. But a decisive Jewish majority in the Jewish areas would guarantee that political and economic control would not be transferred to the Arabs. Moreover, rapid Arab social and economic development would lead to a dramatic curtailment of their birthrate and bring to a more balanced ratio of growth between the two partners. The plan also encourages favoring certain areas over others for economic development, by promoting tax cuts and other benefits, for the sake of a more even population distribution in the Jewish areas. This would alleviate the choking and hazardous concentration of most Israelis today in the coastal plain, in what has grown into the frightening megalopolis of the Dan region, north and south of Tel Aviv.

Weitz did not regard his plan as a permanent solution, but rather envisaged three political alternatives that could develop in the future, and facilitate the transition from his temporary solutions to a more constant outcome. Some of his assumptions of 30 years ago were very close to the realities that have emerged on the ground since:

1 Should there develop an agreement between Israel and Jordan (something that indeed happened in 1994), the three Arab cantons could be annexed to Jordan in one way or another. The plan includes a direct highway to be built between Gaza and Hebron, which does not cross, or run in the proximity of, Israeli towns or villages. Thus, the port to be built in Gaza could become the Jordanian outlet to the Mediterranean, provided no weapons are imported through it, and the Israeli pattern of settlements along the Jordan Valley and the Rafah salient would guarantee the demilitarization of the West Bank and Gaza, respectively, without the need to rely on empty promises in this regard which cannot be monitored.

2 If an agreement with Jordan would turn out to be unfeasible, then Israel should enforce the establishment of the autonomous Arab cantons in any case, and wait for further developments for either affirming the federation of cantons between it and the Arab population west of the Jordan River; or

3 Lead to the establishment of a Palestinian state by uniting the three autonomous Arab cantons into one political entity.

PROBLEMS AND UPDATES
Though Weitz opted for the first alternative of a settlement with Jordan – something that was perhaps possible before the Arab Summits of

the 1970s, when precedence was given to the PLO over Jordan for taking possession of any territory relinquished by Israel – he does not say in what way it was different from the plan proposed by King Hussein in 1972, in his attempt to stem the wave of Palestinian nationalism led by Arafat. In other words, if Hussein could have his way, then why would the Canton Plan constitute any sort of solution at a time when outright federation under the Hashemite Crown was being considered?

A peace settlement between Israel and Jordan was concluded in 1994, but that happened only when Hussein realized that, following Oslo, a Palestinian state, not necessarily amicable to him, was about to be established in his neighborhood, and he wanted to safeguard his flank. In any case, if in the pre-Oslo era the PLO adamantly rejected the idea of federation with Jordan, it would have been even more opposed to one with Israel. Even had the Palestinians agreed to that suggestion, it would no doubt have constituted for them a first step only in their claim to the entire land, once their demography so allowed. For Weitz's optimistic demographic projections, which were to guarantee indefinitely an overwhelming Jewish majority in their areas, could become unraveled if the Palestinians came close to parity or even surpassed the Jews in numbers, and then demanded the revision of the entire federated canton system to respond to the new demographic reality. Events in Lebanon following the civil war of the 1970s and 1980s, when the Maronites lost their prerogatives to Muslim demography, present an encouraging prospect for the Palestinians, but must act as a nightmarish warning to the Israelis.

The Canton Plan was not feasible from the start, not only because it did not provide a permanent solution (in fact it was conceived and devised as a transitional blueprint), at a time when rising Palestinian nationalism on the one hand, and Israel's security plight on the other, demanded one, but because it did not address the basic problems that would have ensued had it been adopted as Israeli policy. For example, what would prevent the Arabs in the cantonal federation to move freely to the overwhelmingly Jewish areas and disturb the demographic balance there? How could Israel unilaterally, in the same federal state, allow the Law of Return for the Jews to be implemented in its cantons, and at the same time prevent the Palestinian right of return from being realized in the Arab areas? The Palestinian areas would likely be flooded by so many returnees as to make the revision of the cantonal system imperative, once the demographic balance had tilted in favor of the Arabs.

In view of the rapid growth of the Arab population, which in spite of massive Aliya to Israel has kept the Arab demographic edge growing (their population doubles every 20 years), the density of the population in the Arab areas would become so unbearable, as to result in overwhelming infiltration to the Jewish cantons (after all it would be within the same federated state), and within one generation or two undo the entire national/ethnic-oriented cantonal system. Moreover, if ethnically, religiously, culturally and linguistically the Palestinians feel a community apart, why would they agree to be part of Israel, unless they were intent on changing its nature and take it over from within?

WHAT LESSONS CAN WE LEARN?

As a professional in the field of development, Weitz addressed mainly the socio-economic aspect of a settlement between Israel and the Palestinians, in line with those who wrongly maintain that economic development is the key to a solution. However, the real world is different, inasmuch as people do not operate according to what seems to us their "economic interest." For, with all due respect to economics, it turns out that what is perceived as "national pride," or the yearning for independence, economic and otherwise, or a religious imperative, often takes precedence over economic development. It is also wrong and counter-productive to try to teach people what is their "best interest", for in the final analysis they know it best.

Therefore, and especially after the Oslo fiasco, where too many concessions by Israel only increased the appetite of the Palestinians and turned those concessions into a launching pad for greater demands, in any future settlement Israel should seek to defend her interests and let others defend theirs. This makes the Canton Plan, which would have undermined the Jewish state and hastened its destruction, not only undesirable, but also obsolete and irrelevant, now that we know what the Palestinians really want. It would have given them the tools to obtain "peacefully" what Camp David II refused to yield to them when their demands for the right of return and Jerusalem became known.

Summary

IT IS EVIDENT THAT in the post-Oslo era and the chaos it has engendered, it is not only urgent and imperative to provide a solution in order to avoid the upheavals inherent in a political vacuum, once the Palestinian Authority has evaporated for all intents and purposes, but it is also vital to generate creative solutions that would avoid the perils of the *status quo* on the one hand and the pitfalls of the Oslo process, on the other. For, if we take cognizance of the fact that the situation today is far more adverse and dangerous, nine years into Oslo, than it was prior to that foolish adventure (that is worthy of inclusion as a concluding chapter in Barbara Tuchman's *March of Folly)* we must come to the realization that a new beginning is necessary, that would scrap all the faults and errors, and circumvent the pitfalls and the traps of the past decade. In order to do that, four new elements must be taken into consideration, which have emerged in Israel, the Middle East and the world scene, as we approach anew the negotiations with the Palestinians and other partners: the rebellion of the Arabs in Israel; the very tangible threats posed to Israel by the emergence of irresponsible powers in the Middle East that wield weapons of mass destruction; the coming to the fore of fundamentalist Islam as a source of belligerency and terrorism; and the new alignments in the world in the aftermath of 11 September, 2001.

THE REBELLION OF THE ARABS IN ISRAEL

The situation of the Arabs in Israel, who total some 20% of the population, has never been easy. However, while for most of their existence in a Jewish-majority state they considered themselves, and were considered by others, as Arabs in Israel, namely as a religious, ethnic, cultural and linguistic minority, the rise of Palestinian nationalism in recent decades, and especially the outbreak of the Intifadah, have forced them to choose between their country and their people, and they have elected the latter. It has become customary for them to claim not only their Palestinian, all-Arab and Muslim (or Christian) identity, but to insist that they are Palestinians, who are also technically "citizens of Israel", while their political loyalty, their sentiments and their national and religious allegiance go to the environing Palestinians, Arabs and Muslims. This unenviable state of affairs, which would be abnormal in any case, gains particular prominence in times of war, when identification with Israel's enemies means for Israelis simply treason, or at the very least suspicion and a mounting sense of distrust towards the beleaguered Arab population of the country.

Lately, two new developments have further exacerbated this situation, and caused the suspicions to erupt into open hostility and accusations towards the Arabs, even though only a small minority of them has been indicted so far. One, has been the growing number of Israeli Arabs who are no longer passive spectators, and possibly supporters and sympathizers of Palestinian terrorism against their own country, but have crossed the perilous red line of direct involvement in those acts including Islamikaze operations that have wreaked havoc on the Israeli population. These acts, not only cause anguish and anger among the Israeli citizenry, which regards the Arabs as only consumers of the tremendous security efforts deployed by the country against terrorism, not as participants partaking of that national striving, but have come to project an image of the Arabs as a de-facto "fifth column" within the gates, who must be guarded against. For not only do they not share in the effort of defense, but they help drain the already over-extended security apparatuses, and thereby deflect them from their primary task of keeping at bay the enemy who knocks at the gates from without.

The other issue that has tremendously alienated the Israeli Arabs and aroused even more suspicion and hostility towards them, is the issue of the Right of Return that the Palestinians have announced as one of the foundation stones of any settlement with Israel. All leaders of the

Arabs of Israel have endorsed publicly this Palestinian ambition, which in effect means flooding the land with so many Palestinian returnees that Israel would simply become a third Palestinian state (after Jordan and the Palestinian Authority if it should persist). For Israelis, this is the utmost proof of the Israeli Arabs' commitment to the annihilation of their Jewish state, if not by direct terror, then by diluting the Jewish population through Arab immigration into the country. Already wide evidence exists of tens of thousands of illegal Arab immigrants into the country, who are aided and sheltered by the Arab citizens of Israel. Therefore, any solution of the Palestinian problem, especially the one advocated in Chapter Ten above, must envisage the inclusion of the Arab citizens of Israel, who claim they are first and foremost Palestinians, within the scope of that solution.

THE EMERGENCE OF IRRESPONSIBLE POWERS IN THE MIDDLE EAST

As conventional wisdom had it, the Palestinians were considered all these years as "the core of the problem of the Middle East", as if a solution for them would automatically bring salvation to the entire region. It has now become evident that the rogue states of the Middle East, especially those included by President Bush in the "Axis of Evil", while exploiting the Palestinian issue to their propaganda benefit, have their own separate agendas: either a quest for power for Saddam, the export of Islam for the Iranians, and delusions of *grandeur* by the Syrians, the Egyptians and the Lybians. Therefore, any solution of the Palestinian issue at the territorial expense of Israel, far from calming the moods in the rest of the Arab world, would on the contrary boost their hopes of delivering the *coup de grace* to a weakened Jewish state that had been forced to retreat to its "natural size", as the Egyptians would have it. Therefore, any solution to the Palestinian issue must seek to guarantee Israeli continued control of a minimal territorial depth that will allow it not only to absorb a first blow, in a situation where its population, defense facilities, troops and industries are judiciously dispersed, but also to regroup and defend itself.

It is clear, then, that in view of the mounting hostility against Israel, not only among the Palestinians, but throughout the Arab and Muslim world, and taking into account the hostile populations that will remain under Israeli control in any case, namely the Palestinians, both in Israel proper and in the Territories, Israel will not be able to relinquish all the territories now under its control, lest its margin of maneuver considerably lowers the threshold of its survivability. This is the reason why the inclusion of Jordan inside the equation will become ever more vital in the future, so as to allow Israel to keep the heights of the West Bank and the Jordan Valley, even as the Palestinian populations there might maintain their political allegiance to the Jordan – Palestinian state envisaged in Chapter Ten.

ISLAM AS A SOURCE OF BELLIGERENCY AND TERRORISM

The rise of militant Islam in the past two decades, and especially after it chose the path of violence and terror, further complicates the dilemmas of Israel, inasmuch as the Muslim fundamentalist movements of the Palestinians, on both sides of the Green Line boundary of Israel, such as Hamas, Islamic *Jihad* and the Muslim Movement in Israel proper, have publicly and ideologically committed themselves to wrest from Israel the entire land of Palestine, which is in their eyes a *waqf* that has been assigned by Allah to the Muslims of all generations to come. It is no coincidence that even during the unjustified euphoria that had seized large portions of the Israelis, the Palestinians and much of the world on the morrow of Oslo, these movements refused to accept any reconciliation with Israel and vowed to bring about its demise. Their efforts to scuttle Oslo were instrumental in the failure of the entire process, even before it became evident that Arafat himself and his Fatah organization were as eager as the Islamists to accept Israel. This means that any settlement of the Palestinian issue, even if accepted by the nominal non-Islamist leadership of the Palestinians, will be rejected by the fundamentalists, who will also strive to annul it.

Already at the end of 2002, two years after the onset of the Intifadah, which seems to be grinding to a halt, out of temporary exhaustion, the Hamas and its associates seems to be gaining parity with the Fatah in public opinion among the Palestinians, which means that no Palestinian leadership would be able, even if it wanted, to ignore them and oblige itself to anything they do not accept. Their popularity stems not only from the collapse of the hoped for peace benefits that never came, but mainly from their adoption of the Islamikaze[1] operations, which have terrified the Israeli public in the past two years, and emerged, in the eyes of the Palestinians, as the ultimate weapon with which they can force the Israelis to surrender. So much so, that even the armed forces of the Fatah, such as the Tanzim and the Aqsa Brigades, adopted the same mode of operation in order not to seem to be lagging behind the Islamists and not to lose their grip on their constituencies as a result. The fact that those same operations are pursued by other fundamentalist Muslims worldwide, such as al-Qa'ida and the Abu Sayyaf group, only lends a universal bent to this mode of struggle and encourages the Islamists to remain adamant in their intransigence.

THE AFTERMATH OF 11 SEPTEMBER, 2001.

While the presence of Islamist groups in the West Bank and Gaza makes it imperative for Israel not to relinquish access and control of their bases, unless they are dissolved and actively prosecuted by any Palestinian authority that might emerge, the worldwide diffusion of Islamic militants in far-flung countries, pushes them beyond Israel's purview and leaves them to the treatment of the US. The latter has herself been severely battered by those elements on 9/11, and has since attempted to combat them almost single-handedly while shaking off the traumas of the Twin Towers and the Pentagon. Hence America's direct interest in the Muslim movements everywhere, and its eagerness to see them arrested or neutralized wherever they are likely to harm its assets or interests. This is her common ground with Israel when it comes to battling terrorism of the Muslim kind, especially the Islamikaze mode thereof.

---

1 For the significance of the term, which combines Islam and Kamikaze, see R. Israeli, "IslamiKaze and their Significance", in *Journal of Terrorism and Political Violence*, 9:3, 96–121, Fall 1997.

America's convergence of interest with Israel does not only emanate from its will to see the Palestinian territories cleaned up of any Islamic terrorist activity, but also to undo the links that exist today between the Palestinian lay leadership and such rogue countries as Iraq and Iran. America has indeed become no less interested than Israel to "reform" the Palestinian Authority and rid it of its corruption, as a condition of American support. Arafat's comradeship with Saddam, and the latter's open support for Palestinian acts of Islamikaze against Israel, tie the Americans directly to the future of the Palestinian entity and its links with other rogue states, which stain it as a rogue entity itself. Thus, no solution is envisaged for the Palestinians, which leaves the issue of the rogue states of the Middle East, including Arafat's Palestinian Authority, as a festering wound.

Contributors to this Volume

Begin, Menachem – the late Prime Minister of Israel (1977–83) and author of the Autonomy Plan for the Palestinians.

Bukay, David – Lecturer in Political Science at Haifa University.

Diskin, Abraham – Professor of Political Science at Hebrew University, Jerusalem.

Hazan, Yakov – the leader of the defunct left-wing Mapam faction, now a component of the opposition Meretz Party.

Israeli, Raphael – Professor of Islamic and Middle Eastern Studies, and a Senior Fellow at the Truman Institute for the Advancement of Peace, all at Hebrew University, Jerusalem.

Marcus, Itamar – Founder and director of the Palestinian Media Watch, Jerusalem.

Nisan, Mordechai – An Arab Affairs specialist and Senior Lecturer at the Rothberg International School, Hebrew University, Jerusalem, and a fellow at the Ariel Center for Policy Research.

Riebenfeld, Paul – the late Professor of Political Science at Columbia University, New York, and one of the founders of the "Jordan is Palestine" Forum.

Stav, Arieh – A prominent author and publicist, Director of the Ariel Center of Policy Research and Editor of the Quarterly *Nativ* (in Hebrew).

Widlanski, Michael – Journalist, columnist and author. Expert on Arab affairs.

Index